How the SCOTS Created CANADA

PAUL COWAN

The Publisher: Dragon Hill Publishing Ltd.

Library and Archives Canada Cataloguing in Publication

Cowan, Paul, 1963–
    How the Scots created Canada / Paul Cowan.

Includes bibliographical references.
ISBN 13: 978-1-896124-10-0
ISBN 10: 1-896124-10-0

    1. Scots—Canada—History. 2. Scottish Canadians—History.
3. Canada—Civilization—Scottish influences. I. Title.

FC106.S3C68 2007   971'.0049163   C2007-900833-X

Project Director: Gary Whyte
Project Editor: Audrey McClellan

PC: P5

CONTENTS

INTRODUCTION 5

CHAPTER 1: HOW THE SCOTS DISCOVERED CANADA 8
    THE TEMPLARS 21

CHAPTER 2: CONQUEST 23
    THE TRUTH ABOUT KILTS AND TARTANS 39

CHAPTER 3: THE FUR MEN 43
    RANALD MACDONALD 60

CHAPTER 4: HOW THE SCOTS SAVED CANADA—TWICE . . . 63
    CULLODEN AND THE HIGHLAND CLEARANCES 79
    CANADA'S FIRST SPYMASTER 82
    JOHN NORTON 84
    THE LADIES FROM HELL 85
    SCOTTISH CANADIAN UNITS 91

CHAPTER 5: THE SCOTS EXPLORE CANADA 92
    HAGGIS 108

CHAPTER 6: NEW WORLD, NEW HOPE 111
    ARCHIBALD MACNAB 127
    RED RIVER BLUES 129
    DONALD MORRISON 134

CHAPTER 7: HOW THE SCOTS CREATED CANADA 138
    CANADA'S LAST DUEL 158
    JAMES MACLEOD 160
    TOP COP 164
    TOMMY DOUGLAS 167

CHAPTER 8: TARTAN RIBBONS 172
    SCOTTISH RAILWAYS 186
    FANTASTIC FLEMING 187
    SCOTTISH GIANTS 189

CHAPTER 9: SCOTCH INC. 192
    STOP THE PRESSES 210
    GUNS, PHONES AND OTHER SCOTTISH INVENTIONS
    AND DISCOVERIES 214
    SCOTS AT PLAY 220

CHAPTER 10: THE HEART IS HIGHLAND 226

NOTES ON SOURCES 239

DEDICATION

To all those, Scots or not,
who left their homelands for a new and better land.

INTRODUCTION

B oasting is not attractive. The claim that the Scots built Canada seems at first to be a prime piece of boasting. Today's Canada is the product of the efforts of literally millions of people. But there is something to the claim that Scots have played a far greater role in creating modern Canada than any other immigrant group.

The foundations of modern Canada were being laid just as the Scots were looking for an outlet for their drive, tenacity and economic ambition. Scotland was too small, and too cramped by English domination of the British Isles, for one of the most educated populations in Europe. Canada offered the perfect setting for them to build a new and better society. For centuries, the Scots had unwittingly been preparing themselves to seize the opportunities waiting for them in the slumbering top half of the North American continent.

They were well used to a harsh climate and hard work. Canada was made for the Scots, and the Scots made Canada.

The Scots took to and dominated Canada in a way they never did the United States, Australia, New Zealand or South Africa. Centuries-old associations with both England and France made the Scots the perfect lubricant between the two clashing cultures in the New World. They were used to being junior partners in bed with an elephant. The Scottish presence ensured Canada did not become just a bigger version of England.

Of course, the Scots in Canada came in all shapes and sizes. Some were crooks, some were racists and some were bigots. But there was an underlying current of tolerance and respect for the rights of their fellow human beings that remains firmly woven into the fabric of Canada.

The Scots were among the first Europeans to set foot in Canada, and they kept coming. Wave after wave followed, and often led, the European settlement of Canada. The Scots spread themselves thinly but thoroughly across the country. In Canada's formative years, Scots controlled the economy, politics and the media. They pushed their far more numerous Irish and English cousins aside to take full advantage of the challenges and chances Canada had to offer. There is no more fearsome sight in the world than a Scotsman on the make. Whether they were running the country or running a country store, the Scots were determined to make both themselves and Canada a success.

Experience with the English made them bitter opponents of what the United States regarded as Manifest

Destiny—inevitable expansion of the U.S.A. throughout North America. Scots played a leading role in repelling two American invasions. They became staunch Canadian nationalists.

For better or worse, the Canada we live in today is a product of Scotland. In this book, I look at some of those nation-building Scots, famous, infamous and, in all too many cases now, just plain forgotten.

The numbered chapters in this book follow a broadly chronological order, although one will often overlap another because of the different subject areas covered in each chapter. Interspersed among the main chapters are a series of short segments that look at some of the individual characters and cultural baggage of the Scots in Canada. Some of these short sections expand on the previous chapter; others are unrelated to any of the chapters and so are spread randomly through the book. It's our hope that these will add to your knowledge of the Scots influence on this great country.

CHAPTER ONE

HOW THE SCOTS DISCOVERED CANADA

We will probably never know who discovered America. The one thing most people now agree on is that it wasn't the blabbermouth Italian explorer Christopher Columbus—the Scots were almost certainly here long, long before him.

The details of the journey from the cradle of humanity in Africa to North America may also never be known. Some people believe the first settlers in North America came across the Bering Strait from Russia tens of thousands of years ago. However, the voyage of a small, leather-hulled boat or *currach* from Ireland to Newfoundland via Scotland in 1976–77 opened up a range of new possibilities. The journey showed that the North Atlantic was not the barrier to travel that many had previously believed.

Before adventurer Tim Severin and his crew reached Newfoundland in the currach, many experts believed a leather boat would fall to pieces in the salty Atlantic swell. Severin proved that the Irish monk St. Brendan and his followers could have crossed the Atlantic in the seventh century. The technology used to build the leather boat was thousands of years old by AD 600, and St. Brendan encountered people settled on several of the North Atlantic islands during his journey, so there may well have been an earlier crossing.

Even if St. Brendan and his Irish crew were the first Europeans to set foot on Canada's shores, a Scottish connection can't be ruled out. In St. Brendan's time, there were close links between Ireland and Scotland. The word "Scot" derives from the Latin "Scotti," which means "Irish sea pirate." The Scotti had been carving out a kingdom in western Scotland since before the Romans left Britain around AD 410. Considering the strong links between Ireland and the kingdom of Dalriada (modern Argyll), it's not unreasonable to believe that St. Brendan's crew included at least one sailor/monk from what is now Scotland. This becomes even more likely when you consider that Scots could have been crossing the Atlantic long before the Romans arrived in the British Isles.

The Scotti were only the latest in a succession of waves of immigrants to turn up in northern Britain after the end of the ice age and the retreat of the glaciers, which allowed human settlement. Among the earliest settlers on the Scottish mainland and the islands to the immediate north and west were the Iberians. It is widely accepted that they were eventually pushed to the very fringes of the British Isles. But could those population pressures have pushed them all the way across the Atlantic?

The North Atlantic is dotted with islands that act as stepping stones for settlers heading west, so it's possible the Iberians crossed that ocean long before St. Brendan made the voyage in a 36-foot leather boat. The Iberians are believed to have been small, dark-skinned people with high cheekbones and coarse black hair. That description fits the Skraelings, the people the Viking sagas describe as living in Vinland (Newfoundland). The language the Iberians spoke vanished almost completely from Europe, but some researchers have linked it to Native American language groups.

Some academics now think that North America was settled from both the east and the west, but the westerners eventually came to dominate the continent. This might explain why the Inuit of the eastern Arctic told archaeologists that the remains of what appear to be stone longhouses had nothing to do with their people but had been built by people from the east. Could these longhouses have been the work of the Iberians or perhaps migrants from what is now northern Norway who colonized parts of Scotland briefly before heading farther west?

In 1999, Canadian writer Farley Mowat reopened the debate on early European settlement in Canada by proposing, in his book *The Farfarers*, that the longhouses had been built by Scottish walrus hunters sometime before St. Brendan's voyage. Mowat dubbed his settlers the "Albans" and speculated that they had been squeezed out of Scotland by the Celtic Scotti pushing up from the south and west and by the Vikings sweeping in across the North Sea. He has the Albans colonizing Iceland and then, when the Vikings arrived there, pushing on to Greenland. When the pesky

Vikings showed up again, the Albans moved into the Baffin Island, Hudson Strait and Ungava Bay areas.

Mowat says that teeming walrus herds along the shores of Arctic Canada attracted the Albans. Walrus tusk was literally worth its weight in gold, and the massive sea mammals also yielded tough, durable hides and oil, which were valuable trade items. Mowat argues that the Albans could have built the low-walled longhouses, most of which are about 45 feet long. According to Mowat, the Albans' walrus-skin boats were also 45 feet long and were used as roofs for the longhouses. To back up this claim, he points to the walrus-skin umiak boats of the Alaskan Inuit, which were capable of carrying 30 people across the Bering Strait and, when overturned on shore, provided temporary shelter for travellers.

Mowat believes the Albans eventually moved south into Labrador and Newfoundland, where they became involved in the fur trade. Many of the Alban settlers intermarried with the other ethnic groups inhabiting the area, but Mowat speculates there was still a distinct Alban community into the early 1500s. As rapacious Europeans started to turn up on the coast of Newfoundland, however, the Albans retreated inland, and the last of them settled in the area of what is now known as King George IV Lake.

It is also possible that the longhouses have nothing to do with any early European settlement. It has only recently been accepted that not every technical advance in North America has to be attributed to mysterious visitors from across the Atlantic. Part of the Scots' success as settlers around the world is a result of their ability to recognize the worth of host cultures and adapt the best practices they find to their own use.

For years, scholars scoffed at the notion that Irish monks or Viking adventurers could have crossed the Atlantic. We now know that it was technically possible for St. Brendan to have made the voyage, and archaeological evidence proves the Vikings had a settlement in northern Newfoundland.

And it is from the Viking sagas that we know the names of the first two Scots in Canada to be identified as Scots. Well, we have the Viking versions of their names—Hake and Hekja. It's doubtful their neighbours back in Scotland knew them by those names. The couple were part of Thorfinn Karlsefni's expedition to Vinland in around 1007.

According to the Viking sagas, Hake and Hekja were "swifter than beasts." When Karlsefni saw a likely spot for his settlement, he put them ashore to check it out. The pair was ordered to return to the expedition's ships within three days. And three days later they came back bearing wild wheat and what many translators of the sagas believe were grapes. The Scots are described as wearing strange one-piece, sleeveless, hooded shirts that fastened between their legs.

Based on what the Scots found, Karlsefni decided to build a settlement and trading post. The sagas say the settlers, which must have included the Scots, spent three years in Vinland.

The Vikings' relations with the Skraelings were checkered. At first they were only seen hovering offshore in their boats, vanishing before any contact could be made. In the spring after the Vikings settled, the Skraelings reappeared and traded furs for red cloth and porridge. The peaceful trade came to an unexpected end when a squinty-eyed, bad-tempered little Viking bull scared the living daylights out of the Skraelings and they fled. Three weeks later they returned, looking for a fight, and from then on the history of the settlement is dotted with accounts of fighting between the Vikings and the Skraelings.

During the Vikings' first year in Vinland, Karlsefni and his wife, Gudrid, had a son named Snorri. Karlsefni was said to have Scottish blood, so Snorri must have had a little, too. Which means that the first recorded birth of a European child in Canada had a Scottish connection.

But the Scottish connection with Viking settlement in Canada goes back father than Karlsefni and the Vinland settlement. According to the sagas, Karlsefni traveled to Vinland because his brother-in-law Leif Erickson, back in Greenland, had told him about the place. Erickson had cruised the coast after hearing of fellow Viking Bjarne Herjolfson's sighting of a mysterious landfall when he was blown off-course during a voyage to Greenland. The sagas say Herjolfson's crew included a Scottish Christian who composed some verses about the voyage, known as "The Song of the Tidal Wave."

Why were the Vikings so keen to have Scots on their voyages across the North Atlantic? Perhaps because the Scots were already recognized for their knowledge and expertise when it came to trans-Atlantic travel.

But the Scots may not have been the only ones crisscrossing the Atlantic. Some Canadians may have been travelling to Scotland long before anyone realizes. The islands north of the Scottish mainland share legends of mysterious seal-men called Selkies. The Selkies were seals that could turn into men—or were they men who could turn into seals? Anyway, they were seals in the water and men on the land, and they reputedly liked to seduce local maidens. Some cynics might suggest that the Selkie legends were just a means to explain away the pregnancies of unmarried women.

But there is another explanation. Imagine a superstitious island peasant's first sighting of a man bobbing offshore in a kayak. The peasant's description might well have included the words "seal" and "man." There are documented reports of men in kayaks being found in Scottish waters in the 1700s. But who knows how long before that these solo wayfarers, possibly blown off-course by storms, had been turning up? Perhaps some of the Orkney men recruited by the Hudson's Bay Company in the early 1700s to work in Canada were returning to the land of their forefathers and didn't even know it.

It's probably safe to assume that the Scots and other Europeans were active along North America's eastern seaboard for some time before professional explorers such as Christopher Columbus and John Cabot turned up in the late 1400s. It was the job of Cabot and Columbus to blow their own trumpets and announce their "discoveries." But only a fool of a businessman would advertise the location of one of the great natural food resources known to man—the fishery on the Grand Banks off Newfoundland.

It is only recently that anyone has known for sure where a ship travels after it leaves port. In the past, ships could return lying low in the water with the weight of fish they were carrying, and no one would know where they had been harvesting the deep. The need for secrecy meant that sailors who had been to the Grand Banks would not speak of their voyages or leave much trace of their temporary camps in

Newfoundland. The Scandinavian settlers in Greenland, last heard of in the early 1400s, and their Inuit partners in the whaling industry must have been aware of the Grand Banks. Who knows how long the fishermen of northern Europe, including Scots from Leith, Berwick and Orkney, had been operating off the Grand Banks before Cabot lowered his bucket into the seething mass of cod that made the water appear to boil.

Some say it was Orkney fishermen who, in the late 1300s, told the Earl of Orkney, Henry Sinclair, about the bountiful land across the western sea where man could be free from persecution. Legend has it that Sinclair was custodian of one of the Western world's great treasures—the Holy Grail—and was looking for a good hiding place for it. The Grail was reputed to be part of a treasure looted from the Temple of Solomon in Jerusalem by the mysterious Knights Templar. When the Templar order was smashed in 1307, the treasure apparently vanished. There are those who believe it was smuggled out of the French port of La Rochelle to Scotland, where it was put into the safe-keeping of the Sinclair, or St. Clair, family.

The Sinclairs first came to Scotland in the 1100s as part of an influx of French Norman knights who were invited in to form the nucleus of an army intended to defend the country from English conquest. The Normans, regarded as the most effective cavalry in Europe, had already conquered England in 1066. The Sinclairs thrived in Scotland and were granted land at Rosslyn, near Edinburgh. Then, through marriage, they gained control of the Orkney Islands, still officially part of Norway at the time, and neighbouring Caithness on the Scottish mainland.

It is said that when Henry Sinclair was looking for a place to hide the Templar treasure, he fixed on a spot along the North American coast. Evidence of Sinclair's supposed involvement in an expedition to North America comes from an Italian manuscript published in 1558 that describes a voyage made by brothers Antonio and Nicolo Zeno in 1398. It mentions a man called Zichmni, who some researchers have identified as Henry Sinclair.

Supporters of the theory that Sinclair sailed to North America, possibly Nova Scotia or Massachusetts, point to carvings in the chapel the Sinclairs built at Rosslyn. The carvings resemble plants, such as maize and aloe vera, that are found in North America but not in Scotland. Supporters also mention a rock carving near Westford, Massachusetts, that is said to show a medieval knight in armour. The arms on the knight's shield are supposedly those of the Clan Gunn, close allies of the Sinclairs, and the broken sword carved on the rock indicates it is the grave of a man killed in battle.

The theory that Sinclair brought the Templar treasure to North America has been given a boost recently by a flurry of books about the Holy Grail and by speculation that the Holy Grail is not the chalice Jesus Christ used at the Last Supper but is proof that Jesus married and had children, whose descendants are alive today. These theories tapped into the North American appetite for tales of conspiracy, secret societies and treasure. Let's just say it makes good commercial sense for authors to come up with North American links.

One focus for supporters who believe the stories of Sinclair and the Templar treasure is tiny Oak Island off the coast of Nova Scotia. Three schoolboys visiting the island in 1795 discovered a mysterious shaft. The three boys—Jack Smith, Daniel McInnes and Anthony Vaughan—were convinced they had found a pirate's treasure hoard. They began digging and, depending on which version of the tale you believe, came across a layer of flagstones and then one or two tiers of logs. The boys stopped digging at around 30 feet and went back to the mainland for help. But no adults wanted to get involved, and several years passed before the three boys, now young men, returned to dig up what was dubbed "the Money Pit."

One day in the early 1800s (the exact date is disputed), the three young men and their financial backers began their excavation, encountering various barriers at 10-foot intervals. They reportedly reached a depth of 100 feet and believed they were about to reveal the treasure. Sadly, they put off the recovery effort until the next morning. When they returned to the shaft, they found it was filled with water to a depth of about 60 feet. It would never be dry again. Depending on whom you believe, human-made tunnels or natural fissures in the rock fed sea water into the shaft.

Several fortunes and six people's lives have been lost in the search for the treasure. Enough people, including future U.S. president Franklin D. Roosevelt, have believed the shaft on Oak Island is part of an elaborate treasure labyrinth to keep the hunt going. In the mid-1800s, Nova Scotia miners were brought in with a hardrock drill that reached the bottom of the shaft and came up with three links from a small gold chain caught in the drill head. Cynics suggest someone keen to ensure continued financing for the treasure hunt planted the links.

The apparent complexity of the tunnel system led enthusiasts to believe it had been constructed by someone with greater resources at hand than a mere pirate captain would have. In the late 1800s, the belief that Henry Sinclair had travelled to Oak Island and directed the construction of the pit began to grow. People claimed he'd even built a small fort on the mainland near Guysborough. The lost treasure of the Templars would justify the elaborate precautions taken to protect the secret of Oak Island. Perhaps the original plans for the treasure labyrinth were the work of Leonardo da Vinci himself. And a powerful noble-man such as Sinclair, with the reputed wealth of the Templars behind him, would have had the resources to build it.

It all made sense...to some people. But it's odd that no one in Orkney, an area with a wealth of legend and lore, had heard about Sinclair's voyage until relatively recently.

Certainly, the boys on Oak Island had never heard of Henry Sinclair. But they did believe a Scotsman had buried the treasure. They thought they had found the fabled treasure of legendary pirate Captain William Kidd.

Poor old Captain Kidd. He's one of the most famous pirates in the world, but he may not have been a buc-caneer at all. His harsh treatment at the hands of the English-dominated authorities in New York was a warning to all Scots in North America not to get above themselves.

Kidd was a prickly, hot-tempered and proud man who was born the son of a preacher around 1645 in either Greenock or Dundee, Scotland. He moved to New York as a young man and enjoyed considerable success as a merchant and sailor. He even managed to marry a rich young widow. He cut quite a figure on the streets of New York and was one of the few citizens who were able to afford a fashionable powdered wig.

Kidd soon found himself employed to hunt down the pirates who plagued the waters off New England, Nova Scotia and the Caribbean. It was no surprise, then, that he was approached by a group of New England merchants and politicians to lead a licensed hunt for enemy (i.e., French) ships in the Indian Ocean.

There was room for private-sector initiative in the wars of the late 1600s and early 1700s. Sea captains were given licences that allowed them to legally intercept ships operated by an enemy country—in the case of British captains, these were usually French ships—and confiscate their cargoes. This "privateering," as it was called, could be a very lucrative business.

Kidd was apparently concerned about the legality of the deal he was being offered in New York but allowed himself to be talked into heading the expedition in a brand-new but badly built ship. The ship was equipped with oars as well as sails, which in theory made it highly manoeuvrable. But it needed an usually large crew, and that was part of Kidd's downfall.

The Royal Navy boarded Kidd's ship shortly after it set sail, and a large portion of the crew was legally shanghaied into naval service. The replacement sailors Kidd found were a rough bunch and almost certainly included some former pirates. When the new crew suggested a little piracy and the captain refused, he had a mutiny on his hands. The short-tempered Scot had little time for the mutineers and brained one of their leaders with a heavy iron-hooped bucket. The sailor died from a fractured skull, and the incident would ultimately be the death of Kidd.

Flags of convenience in the shipping world are nothing new, and in Kidd's time it was often hard to determine whether a ship was French or not. Soon stories were flowing back to New York and London alleging that Kidd had turned pirate. He'd already alienated the Royal Navy, and soon he added the powerful merchants of the East India trading company to his list of enemies. They had little trouble believing the stories of bloody piracy surrounding Kidd. In fact, most, if not all, of the ships Kidd captured appear to have been French, and he was entitled by his privateer's licence to intercept them.

The crunch came when he captured a ship loaded with treasure that was operating with French papers but an English captain. It is said that when Kidd realized the ship had strong English connections, he wanted to let it go. But his mutinous crew, and his backers' demands for a good return from the voyage, persuaded him to seize the ship and its cargo.

Loaded down with the confiscated treasure, Kidd felt he could now return to New York and pay off his backers. On the voyage, Kidd learned he was wanted for piracy. He took the precaution of burying some of his treasure on an island "east of Boston" before he reached New York. Many believe that island lies off Nova Scotia.

Kidd thought he had a deal with the authorities in New England, many of whom were his financial backers for the voyage, and he even told them where to find some of his treasure, which was buried on Gardiners Island in Long Island Sound. The treasure was recovered but Kidd was double-crossed. He was slapped in chains and shipped to London, where he was hanged in 1701 for piracy and the murder of the mutinous crew member.

Kidd wasn't much of a pirate, if he was a pirate at all. His name lives on mainly because of the treasure he reportedly buried. To this day, Oak Island remains one of the focuses for that treasure hunt.

When the Oak Island treasure is recovered, if it ever is, it could well prove to have a Scottish connection. What is beyond a reasonable doubt is that the Scots had connections to Canada long before Columbus and Cabot came on the scene. Were the first Scots in Canada pre-historic refugees, explorer monks, walrus hunters, scouts working for the Vikings, fishermen or a band of knights carrying a secret treasure? Take your pick.

THE TEMPLARS

The Templars originated as a band of nine knights who pledged to protect pilgrims in the Holy Land after the first crusaders recaptured it from the Muslim Saracens. The Poor Fellow-Soldiers of Christ and the Temple of Solomon, to give the group's full name, was founded around AD 1114. Four years later, the crusader king of Jerusalem, Baldwin I, gave the Templars permission to build their headquarters on the site of the ancient Temple of Solomon in the city.

They don't appear to have spent much time protecting pilgrims in those early days. Instead, they tunnelled down into the remains of the old temple. No one knows for sure what the knights found there, but suddenly they became a wealthy organization. Some people believe they found treasure, while others believe they found something far more important. The Templars have been linked to the Holy Grail.

In 1128, the Templars became a religious order of fighting monks that attracted the sons of some of the wealthiest families in Europe. Every one of them signed over his worldly goods to the order. Soon the order was operating a money-transfer business that allowed people to deposit money with the Templars in Europe and reclaim an equivalent sum, less an administration fee, when they reached the Holy Land. The French-based Templars then moved into banking. Their clients included many of the kings and nobles of Europe. But in those days, banking didn't have the staid, respectable image it does now. In 1307, one of the Templars' biggest debtors, King Phillip IV of France, persuaded the Pope of the day to outlaw the Templars for heresy and unnatural sexual practices. The leading Templars were arrested, tortured and killed in various nasty ways.

The order was smashed, but there was little trace of the Templars' reputed treasure. According to legend, it was secretly moved to Scotland, where it and a few surviving members of the order were taken under the protection of the Earl of Orkney, Henry Sinclair.

The Freemason organization, which began as a Scottish trade guild in 1598 and was influenced by the Sinclairs, is said to have incorporated Templar traditions into its rites.

CHAPTER TWO

CONQUEST

T he establishment of New France in the early
1600s offered new opportunities for the Scots,
and at least one Scot may have been in on the
ground floor when Jacques Cartier sailed into the Gulf
of St. Lawrence in 1534. At the time, the ports of
northern France were filled with sailors from across
Europe, and Cartier's crew list certainly suggests
a multinational group. Once the vagaries of spelling
are taken into account, it is possible that Michel Herve
could have been born Michael Harvey either in Scotland or to Scots parents in France. We'll never know.
Jean Rotz, who drew one of the first proper maps of the
St. Lawrence, turns out to have been the son of David
Ross, a Scot who settled in France. (Rotz probably
didn't actually travel to Canada, as the colony on the
St. Lawrence was known, but he would have based
his map on Cartier's charts.)

When Samuel de Champlain's intrepid band of settlers landed on the banks of the St. Lawrence River
in 1608 to found the settlement that would become
Québec City, there was probably a Scot among them.
In 1618, Champlain wrote of a Protestant Huguenot
Scot, unnamed unfortunately, who refused to convert
to Catholicism on his deathbed at the primitive settlement. Champlain himself may well have been born
a Huguenot, which could explain why he tolerated
a non-Catholic at the settlement.

Perhaps the most famous Scot to live in New France
was Abraham Martin. Known as "The Scot," Martin
arrived in Québec City around 1620 and split his time
between farming, fishing and piloting boats on the
St. Lawrence. Martin also fathered nine or ten children with his wife, Marguerite Langlois. The children
included Eustache, who is credited as being the first
European child born in New France, and another son,
Charles, who was one of the first Canadian-born
priests—if not the first. The children counted among
their godparents some of the leading citizens of Québec City at the time, including Champlain himself.
But in such a small community, maybe it's not surprising that the few children had such prestigious
godparents.

Another indication that Martin was a Scot is that he
was one of the two dozen or so settlers in Québec City
who stayed on after the settlement was captured for
England by the Kirke brothers in 1629. It appears this
made him unpopular when the city was returned to
French rule in 1632. The campaign against him cul-
minated in 1649 with a jail sentence for "improper
conduct" with a young girl.

Martin is widely believed to be the "Abraham" who gave his name to the famous Plains of Abraham, where French rule in Canada was effectively ended in 1759 when a British army under General James Wolfe defeated the French and Canadien troops of the Marquis de Montcalm. The 32-acre plot of farmland was sold only a few years after Martin's death in 1664.

Martin's arrival in Québec City coincided with plans to carve out a Scottish colony in the New World. The English had New England, the French had New France and, farther south, the Spanish had New Spain. Scottish nobleman Sir William Alexander suggested the time had come for a New Scotland or, in Latin, Nova Scotia.

The strong political tensions and commercial rivalry between Scotland and England entered a temporary lull when James VI of Scotland succeeded Elizabeth I on the English throne in 1603. Alexander had first come to James's attention as a poet and playwright, and the king put him in charge of screening the hordes of Scots who were making their way to James's court in London at the time, looking for favours from their former countryman. Alexander may also have been a tutor to James's eldest son and heir, Prince Henry, and his work as a royal debt collector in Scotland earned him his knighthood.

Alexander persuaded James to grant him a parcel of land that took in present-day Nova Scotia, New Brunswick, Prince Edward Island and the Gaspé Peninsula in Québec. But he had a far harder time persuading any Scots to move to his proposed colony. For centuries, the Scots had been settling in northern Europe, where they ran successful trading operations and served as mercenaries in the armies of countries such as France, the Netherlands, Sweden and the city states of northern Germany. But crossing the Atlantic to set up a new home in the wilderness was a completely different matter.

Pamphlets were written and recruiters were sent out to find Scots settlers for Nova Scotia. To make the new colony seem more familiar and welcoming, Alexander even renamed several rivers and areas to give them Scottish identities. But all the renaming and flowery descriptions of a paradise across the Atlantic failed to inspire more than a handful of Scots. When the ship hired to carry the colonists to their new home arrived at the southwestern Scottish port of Kirkcudbright in 1622, there were only about 60 people waiting for it.

Bad weather further delayed the expedition, which got as far as Newfoundland before winter set in, making it impossible to colonize Nova Scotia that year. The colonists wintered in St. John's while the ship went back to Scotland for more supplies. When it returned in 1623, two of the key members of the proposed settlement, the blacksmith and preacher, were dead and several other colonists had found work as fishermen. There was already a small Scottish community in St. John's, but it had failed to break the English merchants' hold on the fishing industry, and several Scots had turned to smuggling. It's possible that some of the would-be colonists got caught up in their countrymen's illegal activities.

Eventually 10 of the colonists were persuaded to join the returned supply ship when it left St. John's to spy out a likely site for Nova Scotia's first settlement. It's not clear if they ever set foot on mainland soil (they probably did) before returning to St. John's, where they hitched a ride back to Scotland with a cargo of fish.

One of the major obstacles to Alexander's plans for Nova Scotia was that the French already had a settlement there. What Alexander called Nova Scotia, the French called Acadia. The English did not recognize the French claim and had raided the French settlement at Port-Royal (now Annapolis Royal) in 1613. There were probably 100 French settlers in Acadia at the time, more than there were in Québec City.

By 1623, Alexander had invested about £6000 in his colonization venture but had nothing to show for it. A scheme to create "Barons of Nova Scotia," which was intended to encourage others to invest in the colony, was slow to take off. In exchange for about £150, rich Scots could buy a large parcel of land in Nova Scotia and a lordly title to go with it. When none of the men who bought into the scheme showed any inclination to cross the Atlantic, it was decided to legally designate part of Edinburgh Castle as Nova Scotian soil for the formal granting of the titles.

King James died in 1625, and Alexander was lucky that his successor, Charles I, turned out to be a supporter of colonization. By any standard, Charles was not a good king. He had become heir to the throne when his big brother Henry died and was ill-prepared to take on the job. He sparked a religious war with the Scots by trying to impose an English-style authoritarian church on them, fell out with the English Parliament over the financing of the war, fought and lost two civil wars and had his head chopped off.

But before the affairs of his two kingdoms spun completely out of control, he did establish a Scottish settlement in Nova Scotia. His chance came when war broke out between England and France in 1627. Charles ordered the Kirke brothers to seize New France. The

Kirkes, based in the French port of Dieppe, were of either Scottish or English descent. The French regard them as traitors to this day.

When Alexander protested that the Kirkes' mission interfered with his plans to establish Nova Scotia, a deal was done. The Kirkes' English backers and the Scots under Alexander joined forces to form the Company of Adventurers into Canada. Alexander's son, also called William, became part of the Kirkes' expedition.

The Scots' colonization plan got a boost when the Kirkes intercepted a French supply fleet destined for Samuel de Champlain in Québec City. Without the supplies, Champlain was forced to surrender the settlement to the Kirkes. The Scots managed to build a small fort at Baleine on Cape Breton but were driven out by the French after only two months. William Jr. also managed to capture the French settlement at Port-Royal and establish a colony there. This was possible, in part, because of the collaboration of the de La Tour family, who were leading citizens of Port-Royal. Claude de La Tour had a Scottish wife.

However, the Scottish settlement at Port-Royal did not prosper. The winter of 1629–30 killed off 30 of the 70 settlers, and it was only thanks to the help given, possibly grudgingly, by local Aboriginal people that the death toll was not higher.

The colony at Port-Royal struggled on until 1632, when Charles, who was short of cash, gave it back to the French in exchange for the unpaid half of his French wife Henrietta's dowry. Québec was also returned, and compensation promised to the Alexanders for their losses was never paid. All the family had to show for its trouble was the empty title of Viscount Canada. The title died with William Alexander's last male descendant in 1759—only four years before New France finally fell into British hands.

Of course, the Scots did not disappear completely from Canada between 1632 and 1763. A handful of the settlers in Port-Royal stayed on after French rule was restored, and their descendants were eventually absorbed into the Acadian population. Scottish soldiers fought on both sides as Britain and France played tug-of-war with what one called Nova Scotia and the other Acadia. In 1654, British troops in the service of the republican commonwealth established after the execution of Charles I conquered Acadia. But Charles's son, Charles II, who took the throne following the collapse of the republic, returned the conquered lands to the French in 1667.

The Treaty of Utrecht in 1713 gave all of Atlantic Canada, apart from Cape Breton and some smaller islands, to the British. The first British governor of the restored Nova Scotia colony was a Scot. Samuel Veitch was a survivor of the disastrous Scottish attempt to colonize Panama in Central America. The Darién scheme, as it was called, was sabotaged by King William III and his English backers in 1699. (William was also the king of Scotland at the time.) The failure of the Darién project damaged the Scottish economy so badly that its leading citizens were unable to resist passage of the law that led to the unequal union of the Scottish and English parliaments in 1707.

Veitch had been urging the British to seize all the French colonies in North America since 1707, but it would be more than 50 years before his dream came true. When it did, his fellow Scots played a big part in the conflict—on both sides. To understand why this was the case, it is necessary to take a quick look at what was happening in Scotland at the time.

In 1689, four years after Charles II was succeeded on the thrones of Scotland and England by his brother James II, there was a bloodless coup orchestrated mainly by the English. The coup put William III on the throne alongside his wife, James's daughter Mary. Almost immediately, an army of Highland clansmen tried to put James II back on the throne. Although the High-landers beat a British army at the Pass of Killiecrankie, the battle cost them the life of their commander, Vis-count Dundee, and the rebellion collapsed.

Highlanders provided the backbone for several failed attempts to restore James II and his heirs to the throne in 1715, 1719 and 1745. Each failure sent a fresh wave of Jacobite Scots to France, where many joined the French army to fight against the British in the many wars going on at the time. Soon Scots were facing each other across battlefields throughout the world as the French and British clashed in North America, the Caribbean, India and Europe.

A twist was added when the final Jacobite rebellion was put down following the Battle of Culloden, near Inverness, in 1746. General James Wolfe, who fought the rebels at Culloden and, legend says, refused to join in the wholesale slaughter of the wounded after-ward, suggested that his former foes would be the perfect troops to use in North America. He branded the Highlanders a "secret enemy" in a letter sent to his superiors in 1751 and suggested it would be better if the young men of northern Scotland were fighting the French rather than providing a pool of potential recruits for any further Jacobite rebellion. "They are hardy, intrepid, accustomed to rough country and no great mischief if they fall," he wrote.

The British already had one regiment of Highlanders, the Black Watch, which had fought with some distinction against the French in Europe. The regiment was soon on its way to New York to fight the French in North America. But the Black Watch was drawn from clans that traditionally supported the British government against the Jacobite rebels. Now the British decided to recruit two regiments from clans that had fought against them.

The chief of the Clan Fraser, whose lands had been forfeited after Culloden, was now offered them back if he would raise a Scottish regiment to fight the French. Although no longer a powerful landowner, he had little difficulty recruiting more than 1000 men for the new regiment. The Fraser Highlanders and the third Highland regiment, the Montgomerie Highlanders, were soon on their way to North America as well.

The Highland troops proved adept at the ambush tactics commonly used in the war being waged in the deep forests of North America. Dressed in kilts and, unlike the rest of the British troops, armed with broadswords, they proved worthy opponents of the French and their Aboriginal allies.

In 1758, the Black Watch suffered heavily in a badly planned and executed attack on the French-held fort at Ticonderoga, near the junction of Lake George and Lake Champlain in present-day New York state. The Montgomerie Highlanders also lost many men in an ill-advised attack the same year on Fort Duquesne, at the site of what is now Pittsburgh.

Fort Duquesne plays a role in the story of a Scot who later claimed he changed the course of Canadian history by telling Wolfe about the path leading from the bank of the St. Lawrence River up onto the Plains of Abraham. Captain Robert Stobo was born into a prosperous Glasgow merchant family in 1726. He was sent to Virginia at the age of 16, following the death of his parents, and became involved in the local business community. Like many Scots arriving in North America, before and after, he had family connections to help him in his new home, including Robert Dinwoodie, the governor of Virginia, who was a distant relation. Stobo joined the Virginia militia, and when future rebel and U.S. president George Washington was sent to secure the strategically important Ohio Country in 1754, Stobo went along as a captain.

Washington was surprised and defeated by the French and handed Stobo over as a hostage until some French prisoners were returned. When Stobo was taken to Fort Duquesne, though, he discovered the French already held eight Virginia militiamen who he believed would have made suitable hostages for the return of the French prisoners. Stobo was outraged and angry at the trick he felt the French had played, and he decided to draw a map of the fort. The plan and a highly incriminating letter were smuggled to the British by friendly Natives.

Meanwhile, Dinwoodie had decided not to release the French prisoners, so Stobo's captors moved him to Québec City. The young Scot lived in comfort there and even became involved in business ventures with some of the French officers. However, disaster struck when the British force attacking Fort Duquesne was defeated. Among the papers found on the body of the British commander, General Henry Braddock, was the plan Stobo had drawn. The French sentenced

Stobo to death as a spy, but the French government refused to ratify the execution. Stobo was luckier than some of Braddock's officers, who were burned to death by Native people outside the gates of the fort.

It appears Stobo persuaded his jailers to allow him considerable freedom of movement. After two failed escape attempts, he was finally able to slip away from Québec in May 1759. The escape was made in the company of two other Scots—a fellow Virginia militia officer named Stevenson and a former Leith carpenter named Clarke.

The Scots fled in a birchbark canoe down the St. Lawrence to the Isle aux Coudres, where they shot two Natives to death, supposedly in self-defence. Clarke then scalped the Natives, telling Stobo: "Good Sir, by your permission these same two scalps, when I come to New York, will sell for twenty-four good pounds; with this I will be right merry, and my wife right beau." As scalping is not a traditional Scottish activity, it must be assumed Clarke picked up the habit in America.

The three men then killed the Natives' dog to stop its howling and forced a local French landowner to help them row to freedom. Farther down the St. Lawrence, they captured a small sailboat and managed to trade that for a sailing sloop, which carried them to General Wolfe and his British troops (including the Fraser Highlanders and Royal Scots) at Louisbourg, on Cape Breton Island.

Stobo was not present at the siege of Québec, but he would insist for the rest of his life that it was he who told Wolfe about the best approach to the city. He returned to England, joined the British Army and received a serious head wound while fighting in Cuba. In 1767, he bought land in the Lake Champlain area but then found the legal title was in dispute. Legal troubles, his head wound and anger at the army's failure to promote him are believed to have been responsible for his decision to blow his brains out in 1770. By then, the British were in firm possession of Canada.

Shortly after Stobo reached Louisbourg in 1759, Wolfe and his troops, including the Fraser Highlanders, made their way to Québec City. The Black Watch and the Montgomerie Highlanders were part of the British Army pushing north from New York toward Montréal. It's interesting to note that when the Frasers first arrived in America, they were ordered to discard their heavy kilts and don trousers, but their commander, Colonel Simon Fraser, refused. The Black Watch, however, did fight for part of the time in trousers made out of old tent canvas.

The Frasers' moment of glory came at Québec City. A party of the Highlanders was in the lead boat as Wolfe moved his army upstream for the climb up onto the Plains of Abraham. French sentries on the banks of the St. Lawrence twice challenged the British boats, but on both occasions Captain Simon Fraser of Balnain answered them in their own language and convinced them that what they saw was a supply convoy. Fraser was one of several officers who had fled to France after Culloden.

The Highlanders then led the way up the steep path from the river to the plateau. They climbed by grabbing at tufts of grass, bushes, tree roots and branches. Near the top of the hill, a French sentry challenged the party. Captain Donald Macdonald, another former Jacobite who spent time in France, replied in French and caused momentary confusion that allowed the

Highlanders to overwhelm the French troops at the top of the path.

By morning, Wolfe's whole force of 9000 was lined up on the Plains of Abraham. The Frasers were in the front line when the Marquis de Montcalm, who had given the Black Watch such a licking at Ticonderoga, marched out with his French and Canadien* troops to meet the British. Some say the marquis should have stayed inside the walls of the city.

The British allowed Montcalm's troops to get within 25 yards of them before unleashing a series of devastating volleys of musket fire. The Frasers fired one volley and then threw their muskets aside to charge Montcalm's soldiers with their broadswords. The lack of discipline cost them heavily in terms of casualties, but it terrified Montcalm's men. One Canadien veteran later said the Highlanders were like "infuriated demons."

The French were allowed to retreat behind the city walls, and it was several days before they finally surrendered. By then, both Wolfe and Montcalm had died from the wounds they had suffered in the battle. The new French commander was the Commandant de Ramezay, a descendant of Scottish Ramsays who had gone to France as mercenaries in the 1500s. Among the senior British commanders was Brigadier James Murray, and some accounts have him conversing with de Ramezay in Gaelic after the surrender.

Other Scots on the French side on the Plains of Abraham included the Chevalier de Johnstone (an aide to Montcalm, who fled Scotland after the defeat at Culloden) and at least one member of the Douglas

---

* The Canadiens were the descendants of the original French settlers in the colony of Canada.

family, which had been raising troops for both British and French service for hundreds of years. One of the Jacobite officers captured at Culloden was identified as Charles Joseph Douglas, Comte and Seigneur de Montréal, and several members of the family would have served in New France under the fleur-de-lys. The Frasers were sure there were Scots fighting them at Québec City, and a small group of Highlanders captured in the fighting before that city fell reported being surprised when a French officer began talking to them in Gaelic.

After the French surrender, Brigadier Murray (another Scot who claimed to have told Wolfe how to get onto the Plains of Abraham) was named governor of Québec. The following spring, he led a British army out of the city to face General François Lévis and a fresh French army. The British, weakened by the effects of a severe winter, lost the battle, but the Frasers fought well before joining the general retreat back behind the city walls. Afterward, one of the Frasers, a veteran of Culloden, which was also fought during the month of April, is reputed to have remarked: "From April battles and Murray generals, good God deliver me." This was a reference to Brigadier Murray and his clansman Lord George Murray, who was one of the senior Jacobite commanders at Culloden.

The French might have retaken Québec, but a relief convoy managed to reach the British just in time. Murray then marched his army, which included the Fraser Highlanders, to Montréal to join the troops coming up from the south and complete the British conquest of New France.

Murray returned to Québec to resume his duties as governor. During his term of office, he contributed greatly to creating the Canada we know today. Murray disobeyed instructions to anglicize New France after the British gained full control following the Treaty of Paris in 1763. He refused to summon an assembly that only Protestants, mainly English and American merchants, could vote members into. He surrounded himself with Canadien advisors and did everything he could to see that French legal practice was upheld within the framework imposed by the Treaty of Paris. Although he at first despised the priests of New France and feared the influence they had on the Canadiens, whom he described as "perhaps the bravest and best race on earth," he later came to rely on the Catholic clergy in his battles with the English and American merchants. Murray was the fifth son of a Scottish nobleman, so it is perhaps not surprising that he had more sympathy for the seigneurs and priests of New France than the opportunistic merchants who came north from New England.

His decision to moderate the terms of the Treaty of Paris probably helped ensure Québec's loyalty, or at least neutrality, during the American Revolution. The model of colonial rule he established was later used by the British in their growing empire to deal with conquered people they considered "civilized."

But while he helped preserve the French identity of Québec, Murray has his critics, who argue that his actions retarded the region's development for over 300 years. They charge that Murray's support for the clergy and opposition to commercial interests were two factors that prevented Québec from enjoying the fruits of the economic boom going on in the rest of North America until the Quiet Revolution of the 1960s and 70s.

The merchants certainly resented the laws Murray passed to prevent profiteering and hoarding during

Québec's slow recovery from the years of warfare, and it was their complaints that resulted in Murray being recalled to London to face a charge of obstructing the course of justice. The charge arose from his alleged failure to deal properly with some of his soldiers who attacked a merchant in Montréal. Murray was cleared but never returned to Canada.

Murray may not have made his home in Canada, though he owned some big parcels of land here, but many of his faithful Highlanders did. After taking part in a 1762 expedition to recapture St. John's, Newfoundland, from the French, many members of the Fraser Highlanders decided to settle in the land they had fought to conquer. British policy was to offer land grants in a bid to encourage British soldiers to settle in Canada and provide a core of citizens who were loyal to the Crown and prepared to defend its interests. Although the offer was made to all British soldiers who fought in Canada, it was mainly the men of the Frasers, the Montgomeries and the Black Watch who took up the land grants. Perhaps by the early 1760s many had seen that the old Highland way of life was doomed by new economic realities and social change.

It was once believed that no fewer than 300 Fraser Highlanders took their discharge in Canada, but documents found recently in the Public Archives of Canada put the actual figure at just under 160. Some of the Scotsmen stayed in Québec, where they married local women; others took land grants in Prince Edward Island and Nova Scotia. Former members of the Black Watch also settled in PEI.

Two former officers from the Fraser Highlanders bought Brigadier Murray's estate at Mount Murray, on the banks of the St. Lawrence between Québec

City and Tadoussac, and they encouraged members of the regiment to join them. A successful salmon fishery helped support the ex-soldiers and their families for many years.

Gradually the descendants of the Highland soldiers were absorbed into francophone society, but visitors to communities along the St. Lawrence in the late 1800s noted with surprise that bagpipes were often produced and played during local celebrations and festivities.

THE TRUTH ABOUT KILTS AND TARTANS

There's a lot of nonsense spoken and written about kilts and tartans, so here are some of the straight goods. Or as straight as one person can get them through the tartan myths.

First of all, nothing is worn under the kilt. It is all in perfect working order. But wearing nothing under the kilt does present a little problem in many parts of Canada. It means that one of the most sensitive parts of the male anatomy is exposed to nasty little biting insects. There's something a bit bogus about those paintings of pipers in kilts standing in the prows of fur traders' canoes, playing away on their instruments.

The legendary 78th Fraser Highlanders steadfastly refused to switch their kilts for trousers during the six years they spent fighting the French in the late 1750s and early 1760s. But when many of them took up arms again to expel the Yankee invaders in 1775 as members of another kilted regiment, the Royal Highland Emigrants, they cheated. To defeat the bloodthirsty swarms of mosquitoes and blackflies, they wore canvas shorts that reached down under their kilts to the tops of their knee socks, where they were tied off for a perfect seal.

In 1815, when the 93rd Highlanders, the most Highland of the Highland regiments in the British Army, went into the swamps of Louisiana to teach the Americans a lesson for invading Canada, they wore tartan trews (tight-fitting trousers), not kilts. Probably the last soldiers to fight in kilts in North America were members of the 79th New York Volunteer Infantry during the opening battles of the American Civil War. The Union regiment modelled itself on the British Army's 79th Cameron Highlanders, but as the war progressed, the kilts vanished and the volunteers took on the standard Union uniform.

There used to be two kinds of kilt: the *feilidh-beag* (Gaelic for "small wrap"), ancestor of the carefully tailored article that we know today, and the full *feilidh-mhor* ("big wrap"). About the only people you see wearing the *feilidh-mhor* today are re-enactors of the American Revolutionary Wars. Or perhaps people pretending to be Mel Gibson in *Braveheart* (though despite the movie costume designers' fancies, the *feilidh-mhor* didn't come into use until almost 300 years after William Wallace died).

The dimensions varied, but the *feilidh-mhor*, or belted plaid, was made from a large blanket-sized piece of heavy wool cloth. When it was belted at the waist, the lower part was recognizable as a kilt while the upper section was drawn over one or both shoulders. This formed a primitive backpack, and there were even two pockets formed at the front where the cloth hung over the belt. When it rained, wearers could pull some of the cloth over their head to form a hood. And, of course, it served as a warm blanket at night.

The *feilidh-mhor* was the perfect garment for a poor Highlander living in a cool, damp climate, and it was the peasants of the north and west of Scotland who wore kilts. The rich gentlemen of the Highlands preferred trews. And the Lowlanders, for whom the Highlanders were as alien as Afghan tribesmen, wouldn't be caught dead in a kilt of any kind. In fact, from 1746 to 1782 it was illegal to wear a kilt at all—unless it was as part of a British Army uniform. It was only after Highland culture had been smashed and no longer posed a threat that the kilt became a Scottish national symbol.

The kilt we all know and love today is basically a cut-off *feilidh-mhor* with everything above the belt gone. Some say that an Englishman invented it, but that is not true. In the 1730s, an Englishman named Thomas Rawlinson certainly did encourage the employees at his iron smelter plant in the Highlands to wear the *feilidh-beag* as it was easier to work in. But there's plenty of evidence that people were wearing the cut-off kilts long before that. And it was an easy step from the cut-off *feilidh-beag* to stitching in the pleats at the back permanently.

The kilt, which is basically a double layer of thick wool cloth all around, is a very warm garment. It heats the lower body far faster than trousers do. Certainly, the Fraser Highlanders survived several severe winters in Canada with only their kilts for protection. They had a little help from the nuns of the Ursuline convent in Québec, who knitted them thick woolen knee socks to replace the far less warm canvas hose they had been wearing. But there was little the nuns could do to stop Highlanders destined for guard duty in the Lower Town from sliding down the steep hill on their bare backsides.

Tartan patterns predate kilts in history, but most of the ones we know today were invented in the mid-1800s. The link between tartans and certain families dates from around the same time. Before the kilt was outlawed in 1746, the colours used in tartans depended on which natural dyes were available in a certain part of the country, though wealthier people could afford more and brighter colours in their tartan clothing. If you could work out from the dyes used which part of the country a person was from, you might be able to guess their clan, but that was the extent of the tartan's significance. The Highland officers captured at Culloden often had jackets, waistcoats and either kilts or trews in a clashing array of different tartans that would set the teeth of today's fashion fascists on edge.

It was only when tartan became a fashion accessory in the 1820s, thanks mainly to the British royal family, that "traditional" clan tartans made their appearance. Two of the leading designers were the Polish brothers John and Charles Sobieski Stuart, who published a book of tartans in 1842. Several well-known clan tartans today are actually based on designs commissioned for British Army regiments.

If you want to wear plaid, the best advice is to go with the pattern you like most. There are many Canadian tartans to choose from, including Alberta, Boucherville, British Columbia, Bruce County, Canadian Centennial, Confederation, Essex County, Hudson's Bay Company, Manitoba, Maple Leaf, New Brunswick, Newfoundland, North Vancouver Island, North-West Mounted Police, Nova Scotia, Ontario, Ontario North, Ottawa, Plaid de Québec, Prince Edward Island, Royal Canadian Air Force, Tartan de Laval or Yukon.

CHAPTER THREE

THE FUR MEN

Stretching Canada's boundary all the way west to the Pacific was a brutal business, and much of the path was stained with Scottish blood. It was the Scots-dominated fur trade that pushed European Canadians west toward the Rockies and launched a 30-year turf war that makes many of today's drug gangs look like a bunch of Sunday school kids. Ever since French explorer Jacques Cartier sailed up the St. Lawrence in 1535, furs had been a crucial part of the Canadian economy. By the 1650s, French fur traders were operating as far west as the Great Lakes. But the pelt business really took off after the French surrendered New France to the British in 1763.

The London-based "Company of Adventurers of England trading into Hudsons Bay" had been operating from a chain of forts on the shores of that great inland sea since the early 1670s. Charles II granted the company exclusive rights to all of the land along the rivers that drained into Hudson Bay and made it the absolute ruler of 1.5 million square miles known as Rupert's Land. The French did not recognize the right of a king in London to make such a large land grant, and the forts on Hudson Bay changed hands several times before British tenure was finally recognized in the 1713 Treaty of Utrecht.

The Hudson's Bay Company owed its existence to two renegade French fur trappers who fell foul of the authorities in New France and decided to take their pelts to London, but from the beginning the company had a Scottish connection. One of the French trappers, Médard Chouart, Sieur des Grosseilliers, was married to a daughter of Scot Abraham Martin (the Abraham Martin of Plains of Abraham fame). Even though the company's original shareholders were leading members of English society, canny Scots, such as John Nixon, who became the company's overseas governor in 1679, were soon buying shares in it.

The Scottish character of the Hudson's Bay Company (HBC) received a major boost when the HBC began recruiting men from the Orkney Islands to work at its trading posts in the early 1700s. Until then, the HBC's clerks and labourers had come from the slums and orphanages of London, but life in the sub-Arctic did not agree with the young Englishmen and they proved disappointing employees. For decades, HBC ships had been calling at the Orkney port of Stromness to fill up with fresh water and other supplies before the trans-Atlantic crossing, and they soon began taking on local men to work at Hudson's Bay. The Orcadians were used to living in harsh conditions, were better educated than their English counterparts and, being farming fishermen, were handy on both land and water. The Scots' steady, almost plodding, but dogged approach to life made them good employees. They were also, noted one of their English bosses, "the slyest set of men under the sun."

For many years, HBC traders were content to wait for the Native trappers to bring pelts to them at their trading posts squatting on the shores of Hudson Bay. After the French surrendered New France in 1763, the traders believed complete control of the fur trade would fall into their hands. They were wrong. Instead, buccaneering Scottish traders based in Montréal stepped into the vacuum created by the departure of their French counterparts and began building a Scottish-run empire that would reach the Pacific. Much of the Montréal merchants' empire was carved out of land that was officially part of the Rupert's Land grant to the HBC, including what would later become North Dakota, Minnesota, northern Ontario, Manitoba, Saskatchewan, Alberta and part of the Northwest Territories. The Scottish traders didn't care about the HBC's land claims and proved far more formidable foes than the French had ever been.

There were fortunes to be made in fur. Scot Thomas Curry made enough money from two winters trading on the Saskatchewan River in the early 1770s to retire a wealthy man. It took fellow Scot James Finlay five years to amass his fortune. But in the lawless western wilderness, anything went. Trappers vanished, never to be seen again; trade goods were stolen or dumped in lakes; fur consignments were hijacked. The anarchy was proving to be bad for business, though, so rival Scots traders decided to put an end to it by becoming partners. Soon those partnerships were operating under the umbrella of the North West Company.

The mastermind and driving force behind the North West Company was Simon McTavish, the son of an officer in the Fraser Highlanders who had served with General James Wolfe on the Plains of Abraham. The young McTavish arrived in New York in 1764, and he quickly became involved in the fur trade around Detroit, along with fellow Scot James Bannerman. (They were not the only Scots active in the fur trade at that time. Alexander Henry had traded on Lake Michigan, disguised as a Canadien voyageur, in 1761 and was granted a formal fur-trading monopoly for Lake Superior in 1765.) As the fur supply diminished because of overtrapping, the hunt for pelts moved farther and farther west. Greater distances involved greater investment, and McTavish was soon involved in joint ventures with Canadien Jean Baptiste Cadotte and the Frobisher brothers from Yorkshire. Through share manipulation, McTavish, in his partnership with the Frobishers, came to control the growing alliance of independent fur traders. The brains of the operation in the early days was Benjamin Frobisher, but when he died in 1787, McTavish had learned enough about the business to take control of the joint company and push forward the North West Company's claim to be lords of the lakes and woods of western Canada.

The Montréal-based fur business was split between the wintering partners, who traded pelts in the west, and the businessmen in the east who shipped trade goods to the western end of Lake Superior and took the furs back out. Gradually, thanks to McTavish's influence, the Scots came to dominate the fur business. In 1783, the Frobishers and McTavish had six partners: three Scots, an Irishman, a Canadien and an American. By 1804, only six of the 46 partners in the enlarged North West Company were not Scots or of Scottish descent.

In the early days, the Nor'Westers' main rival was not the HBC but the Glasgow firm of Gregory, McLeod and Co. The Glasgow company's wintering partners included James Finlay's son James Jr., John Ross and cousins Alexander and Roderick Mackenzie. However, when John Ross was murdered by a rival Nor'Wester in 1787, Gregory, McLeod and Co. realized it could not recover from the blow and quickly agreed to a merger with the North West Company.

Other fur trade takeovers were less violent. The Aberdeenshire firm of Forsyth and Richardson was brought under the Nor'Wester umbrella comparatively peacefully, and the glens of northeastern Scotland proved a fertile recruiting ground for the fur trade. One of the first Scots to trade in the Michigan area was William Grant of Trois-Rivières, who came from the same area as two Scots—Donald Smith and his cousin George Stephen—who played a major role in shaping 19th-century Canada. Smith, who would end his life as Lord Strathcona, came to Canada as a fur trader.

Simon McTavish was keen on keeping business in the family. He married into the well-established Canadien fur-trading family of Chaboillez and hired one of his cousins in London, John Fraser, to market Canadian furs and arrange the shipment of trade goods from England. His nephew William McGillivray was groomed as his successor as uncrowned king of the Canadian west. McTavish certainly believed himself to be some kind of royalty, and his partners, and rivals, commonly referred to him as "The Marquis."

In Montréal, McTavish and his partners lived like kings and entertained on a lavish scale. One of their guests, the young New York writer Washington Irving, author of "The Legend of Sleepy Hollow," recorded his impression of dining with the Nor'Westers: "The tables in the great banqueting hall groaned under the weight of game of all kinds; of venison from the woods, and fish from the lakes, with hunters' delicacies such as buffaloes' tongues and beavers' tails....There was no stint of generous wine, for it was a hard-drinking period, a time for loyal toasts, bacchanalian songs and brimming bumpers."

In the spring, the wintering partners would descend on Grand Portage at the western end of Lake Superior—officially on U.S. soil, but the Nor'Westers didn't care about that—and wait with their cargos of fur for the 40-foot supply canoes that brought the eastern partners and supplies for the following winter from Montréal. What followed was part annual general meeting and part massive party. Bagpipers and fiddlers played until dawn as Scots traders and Canadien voyageurs danced with their Native wives and girlfriends in the main hall of the trading fort. Eventually the fort was moved into Canadian territory at Thunder Bay and christened Fort William.

In his novel *Astoria*, Irving described the Montréal-based Nor'Westers as resembling "sovereigns making a progress: or rather like Highland chieftains navigating their subject lakes. They were wrapped in rich furs, their huge canoes freighted with every convenience and luxury, and manned by Canadien voyageurs, as obedient as Highland clansmen....The councils were held in great state...alternated by huge feasts and revels, like some of the old feasts described in Highland castles....Such was the North West Company in its powerful and prosperous days, when it held a kind of feudal sway over a vast domain of lake and forest."

By the early 1780s, the HBC had roused itself from its self-imposed slumber on the shores of Hudson Bay and begun building trading posts in western Canada. The Nor'Westers and the HBC men held each other in contempt, with the HBC men referring to their rivals as "peddlers," and the Nor'Westers branding the Bay men "The English." Fist fights, knife fights and even the occasional murder of a rival trader became the order of the day. The Native people were persuaded, and sometimes intimidated, by traders from one firm to boycott the other.

The relationship between the Scots traders and the Natives was complex. Both groups depended on the other for their living, and both shared a desire to keep white settlers out of the fur country. Many traders, both HBC men and Nor'Westers, had Native wives. The sons of these "country" marriages often found work with the fur companies when they were old enough, but few received promotions. The daughters became wives for the next generation of traders. The marriages taught traders more about Aboriginal culture and customs than they might otherwise have learned and also kept them honest. They were less likely to rip off their father- or brothers-in-law than a total stranger.

The HBC had taken a firm stand against trading alcohol for furs, but the Nor'Westers looked on rum and whisky as staples of their business. A whole season's catch of pelts could be exchanged for just one small barrel of rum. No one will ever know how many Native people were killed in drunken brawls among themselves outside the wooden palisades of the trading posts after being paid in liquor. Traders were careful not to be caught up in the brawls, but the work was still dangerous. In 1811, Murdock Cameron, the Nor'Westers' man in Minnesota, was murdered by the Sioux.

The partners in the North West Company were constantly bickering despite, or perhaps because of, McTavish's imperious hand on the levers of power. A New North West Company was formed in 1800 and included the by then famous transcontinental explorer Alexander Mackenzie among its partners. The new company marked its bales of furs with the letters XY, and many people knew it by those initials. The hatred the Nor'Westers felt for the HBC was shifted to what McTavish dismissed in public as "The Little Company," and the forests and portages of the Canadian west were soon rocked by a fresh wave of violence. But a downturn in the fur business, caused by the loss of markets in mainland Europe because of the seemingly endless war with the French, and the death of McTavish in 1804 led the rebel partners back to the Nor'Wester fold. McTavish was succeeded, as many predicted he would be, by his nephew William McGillivray.

The trade war between the Nor'Westers, mainly Highland Scots, and the Orcadians of the HBC was soon back in full swing. In 1809 at Eagle Lake, Nor'Wester Aeneas Macdonnell chased the Natives from the HBC post and took their furs. The Orcadian boss at the post shot Macdonnell dead.

That same year, the HBC hired former Nor'Wester Colin Robertson to help it beat its rivals at their own game. Robertson advised his new bosses, "When you are among wolves, howl!" Fur cargos belonging to both companies were soon being ambushed and stolen regularly. The Nor'Westers intimidated the Natives into boycotting the HBC trading posts in the Athabasca country, then upped the stakes by seizing the furs that the Orkneymen had collected. Robertson arrived with 200 men and recovered the furs. He was then "arrested" by the Nor'Westers but managed to escape during the journey to Montréal for trial.

Robertson believed his work in the Athabasca country was enough to earn him the HBC's top job. But a dark horse with better family connections to the major shareholders in the HBC pipped him at the post. George Simpson was another tough customer, but he had more polish and business sense than his rival Robertson. "The North West Company are not to be put down by prize fighting, but by persevering industry, economy in business arrangements and firm maintenance of our rights, not by fists but by more deadly weapons," he declared. The board of governors liked what the young Scot had to say about closing down unprofitable trading posts and other business rationalizations.

Economics were certainly on the side of the far less flamboyant HBC. It could ship its furs out of Hudson Bay, which was closer to the prime pelt areas, while the Nor'Westers were stuck with the longer and more expensive route via the Great Lakes and Ottawa River. The HBC was also prepared to play a longer game in terms of returns on investment. When the main partners in the North West Company were taking dividends of £400 per share out of the company each year, the HBC was paying out next to nothing.

By the 1820s, cutthroat competition meant both companies were in financial difficulties and the time had come for them to join forces. But even though the Nor'Westers brought 97 trading posts into the new company to the HBC's 76, the HBC's stronger financial position gave it the whip hand, and what was billed as a merger turned out to be an HBC takeover. George Simpson became the North American leader of the enterprise.

One of Simpson's first tasks was to organize a "celebration" of the merger at Fort William. Many of the traders forecast that blood would be spilled when the Nor'Westers and the Bay men met. Several entered the great hall bearing scars from recent confrontations between the rival firms. Simpson went out of his way to make sure the bitterest enemies found themselves sitting next to each other for the banquet and trusted alcohol to do the rest. It was a gamble that could have resulted in an unprecedented bloodbath on the shores of Lake Superior, but it paid off as foes became friends during exuberant banqueting.

Simpson, noted in later life for his shining, bald head and florid face, pushed the employment of Scots in the fur trade farther than ever before. Simpson favoured recruiting farmers' sons and urged special consideration be given to applicants from Speyside. In the 50 years following his appointment, 171 of the 263 senior traders and officials hired were Scots, with 59 Englishmen, 22 Irishmen and 11 Canadiens completing the roster. Almost 65 percent of all HBC employees in this period were Scots, with 40 percent of them coming from Orkney.

The high number of Scots can be explained by several factors. Thanks to widespread elementary schooling in Scotland, aimed at making sure every head of household could read the Bible, Scots were generally better educated than their English and Irish counter-parts. The Scots faced grimmer economic prospects in Britain than the English and were more motivated to make a success of life in Canada. Widespread poverty and the rain-swept climate in northern Britain had accustomed them to harsh living conditions. They were more prepared to work alongside the Canadiens and Natives than their English counterparts. Finally, and perhaps most importantly, many already had family working in the fur trade. The names McTavish, McGillivray, Mackenzie, Fraser, Grant, Cameron, Mac-Donald, Flett, Inkster, Isbister and Linklater were over-represented in the fur traders' hall of fame.

Simpson was a bastard, both literally and figuratively. He was brought up by relatives in Dingwall, just north of Inverness, and received a reasonable education before gravitating into the HBC thanks to family contacts. The Canadiens dubbed him "The Iceman," and other employees branded him a despot. Most called him "The Emperor." As the HBC's top man in British North America, the barrel-chested Simpson ruled Rupert's Land and its 12,000 Aboriginal, Métis and white inhabitants with the powers of an absolute monarch. He made frequent marathon canoe trips around his domain and acted as both judge and jury in criminal and civil cases. Simpson applied the principles of Scottish law in his judgments rather than the English law used in English-speaking Canada. Scottish law is closer to the French civil code than English common law and, at least in theory, demands a higher standard of proof in criminal cases than its English counterpart. This can result in a certainty of guilt without enough evidence to allow a legal conviction, a situation that generally leads to the unusual verdict of "Not Proven," which basically means, "We know you did it but we've got to let you go; don't do it again."

Simpson travelled the western wilderness with an entourage of up to 30 people, which included his own personal bagpiper, a doctor, servants, clerks and a detachment of armed men. In his early days in Rupert's Land, Simpson had an eye for the ladies and fathered numerous children during brief "country marriages" with Native women that marked his tours of inspection. Some of his children he made provision for, some he didn't. He encouraged his traders to take "country wives," but after he married an 18-year-old cousin when he was in his 40s, he made it clear these Native women were no longer welcome in his presence on social occasions. Traders who wanted promotions soon realized they needed white wives, and the links between the fur men and their Aboriginal partners in the business began to unravel.

Simpson was obsessed with the bottom line. Profit was everything. In the 40 years he ran the HBC, the traders never got a pay rise. He kept a coded note-book in which he detailed the faults of every single one of his traders and senior officials—and he was brutal in his appraisals.

The biggest challenge Simpson faced was the Americans' dream of annexing the whole Pacific Coast. Welsh explorer David Thompson, an employee of the Nor'Westers, arrived at the mouth of the mighty Columbia River in 1811 to find a group of Scottish fur traders working for New York-based John Jacob Astor got there first after sailing around the tip of South America, beating him to the prize by less than four months. A few years earlier, Simon McTavish's nephew Simon Fraser had followed the raging river that now bears his name nearly all the way to the Pacific. Simpson realistically decided that the Fraser rather than the Columbia would probably mark the Pacific boundary of British North America.

At one point it did seem possible that the Columbia would mark the border. In the War of 1812, a group of Nor'Wester traders, led by William McGillivray's brother-in-law John McDonald and cousin John McTavish, seized Astor's fort at the mouth of the river and renamed it Fort George. Astor then sold the fort to the Nor'Westers, and they remained in possession of it after the war ended, though they felt it diplomatic to fly the Stars and Stripes from the fort's flagpole.

Although the Canada-U.S. border from the Great Lakes to the Rockies was set at the 49th parallel, the status of the Oregon Territory, as the land to the west of the Rockies was called, was left hazy. A final decision on the boundary was put off until 1828, and even that deadline was extended. As long as there was no large-scale white settlement, the HBC held sway. Simpson wanted to use the Oregon Territory as a buffer against American expansion that could be traded away if or when the time was right, and he and his men were ruthless in sabotaging attempts by American companies to establish themselves on the Pacific coast. The HBC soon enjoyed a stranglehold on trade in the Oregon Territory. But then the HBC man on the spot gave the Americans an inch—and they took way more than a mile.

John McLoughlin, like many of the leading men in the fur trade, was a grandson of one of the Fraser Highlanders who settled in Québec after fighting on the Plains of Abraham. He studied to be a doctor but fled west in 1803 after a fist fight with an influential

British Army officer. His Fraser contacts soon found the fiery-tempered young man a job with the North West Company, and he played a part in the merger with the HBC. He appears to have kept his rage in check most of the time, but after Clallam people killed five of his traders, he killed about 25 of them and burned their village.

When 900 American settlers turned up to colonize Oregon's Willamette Valley, HBC policy was not to welcome them with open arms. But when they began to starve during the winter of 1842–43, McLoughlin opened the company warehouses to the settlers and extended more than £6500 in credit, which Simpson charged against McLoughlin's personal account with the company.

Relations between Simpson and McLoughlin had been deteriorating since the HBC supremo wrongly ruled that the 1841 shooting death of the doctor's son at a trading post in Alaska was justifiable homicide. After their first meeting in 1824, Simpson had recorded in his secret notebook that McLoughlin was not the kind of man he'd like to meet alone on a dark night and that he wore "clothes that had once been fashionable, but now covered with a thousand patches of different colors, his beard would do honor to the chin of a Grizzly Bear." Both men had personal bagpipers.

The Willamette settlers were followed by more Americans, and it was soon obvious that their government would never surrender the colonists to British rule. Boots on the ground, or rather ploughs on the land, meant the Oregon Territory would be American. Simpson never forgave McLoughlin for letting the American settlers get their foot in the door, and

McLoughlin eventually threw his lot in with them and became a U.S. citizen.

Simpson moved the HBC's Pacific headquarters from Fort George to Fort Vancouver (in present-day Washington state), but even that wasn't far enough north. After a couple of false starts, the HBC decided to establish new headquarters on the southern tip of Vancouver Island, and the British government in London granted the HBC a 10-year lease of the island on condition that the company encourage settlement there. Simpson chose fellow Scot James Douglas to decide on the post's location in 1842.

Work began on Vancouver Island's Fort Camosun the next year. The name was soon changed to Fort Victoria in honour of the British queen. The British sent out their own governor for the Vancouver Island colony in 1849, but he resigned when he realized Douglas was already doing the job perfectly well.

Douglas, like Simpson, was illegitimate, born in 1803, the son of a Scottish sugar plantation owner and his Creole mistress in the Caribbean. After being schooled in Scotland, he joined the North West Company in 1819 and was posted to Fort William. There his hot temper led to a duel with fellow employee Patrick Cunningham. The incident didn't do his career any harm, and at the age of 18 he was entrusted with sole charge of a small trading post. By 1828, he was ready to quit his job in the BC Interior because of the isolation, starvation (once the salmon stopped running) and constant hostility of the local Natives. A pay increase from £60 to £100 a year persuaded him to stay.

The tall, dark-skinned Scot became one of McLoughlin's protegés, but his temper kept getting him in trouble. When Douglas killed an Aboriginal murder suspect in the middle of the man's village, his rashness almost cost him his life. Only the intervention of Douglas's Métis wife saved him.

The Native people on the Pacific coast and in the BC Interior proved far more troublesome than their counterparts east of the Rockies. When Songhees people killed some HBC oxen on Vancouver Island, Ross-shire man Roderick Finlayson demanded they reimburse the company. The Natives laid siege to Fort Victoria in protest. Finlayson brought the uprising to a sudden halt by blasting an Aboriginal lodge to smithereens with a single cannon shot. In 1840, Scottish trader John Tod was faced with 300 hostile Natives in the BC Interior. He defused the situation by calmly announcing that there had been a smallpox outbreak and he needed to immunize everyone with a cut on the arm from his knife. The ruse worked. Scot Sam Black was not so lucky. He was shot dead by a member of the Shushwap band who believed Black's "evil eye" was responsible for the death of a local chief. The killer was handed over by the Shushwap but was shot while trying to escape his white captors.

However, the biggest threat still came from the Americans. When large quantities of gold were discovered along the Fraser River in 1858, more than 15,000 American prospectors flooded up to the mainland from California. When they came through Victoria, they transformed it from a sedate British settlement into a rip-roaring mining squat. It looked for a time as though there was going to be a rerun of the Oregon Territory disaster, with the Americans claiming the land by virtue of overwhelming numbers of settlers. But Douglas and his boss Simpson had learned their lesson, and the Americans were made aware from the moment they entered British territory that they were guests of the Queen. British Columbia was no Texas, and Victoria was not the Alamo.

Mainland British Columbia and Vancouver Island were separate colonies for a time, but Douglas was governor of both, and he ensured British sovereignty in British Columbia by appointing Judge Matthew Baillie Begbie to impose law and order. One of the first things Begbie did was lead a small force of British soldiers, drawn from the Royal Engineers, up the Fraser Valley to the gold fields. There he laid down the mining and immigration laws he had drawn up for the fledgling province to the Yankee prospectors. They, in return, smeared his reputation by describing him as an autocratic hanging judge, but the reality is that by 1871, he had sentenced only three white men to death. During the same period, Begbie sent 22 Natives to the gallows but issued 11 reprieves. No white men were reprieved.

In 1865 alone, Begbie travelled 3500 miles with his circuit court, bringing British law to British Columbia. Sometimes he held court in a shack, sometimes sitting on a tree stump, and on occasion he delivered his judgments from the back of a horse, but he always wore his judicial robes to hear a case. He even carried the small, black cap that British judges traditionally wear to deliver a death sentence. Begbie became fluent in the Shuswap and Chilcotin languages, and he ensured that widowed "country wives" had the right to a share in their dead husband's goods. He also spent years fighting and diluting anti-Chinese laws passed in the province.

Between them, Douglas and Begbie did more than any other two men to ensure Canada had an outlet onto the Pacific. Douglas died in his beloved Victoria in 1877, having lived to see BC become part of the Canadian Confederation. Begbie lived until 1894 and also died in Victoria.

Douglas's mentor, George Simpson, died with the taste of defeat on his lips. He tried unsuccessfully to block a British government move to open the west up for settlement by forcing the HBC to sell Rupert's Land. He announced his retirement in 1859 and was dead the following year. Simpson was the last of the fur traders who could claim to hold dominion over all the lakes and woods of the west.

Canada was changing and changing fast.

RANALD MACDONALD

There was a time when the Hudson's Bay Company was such a big multinational operation that it sent its own spies abroad. One of those spies was Scot Ranald Macdonald, who became the first person to teach the Japanese to speak English.

Macdonald was born when the HBC still controlled what would later become the states of Washington and Oregon in the United States. He was the son of fur trader Archibald Macdonald and Chinook princess Raven. Macdonald's mother died when he was young, and he went away to school in Winnipeg when he was 10. He obeyed his father's wishes and trained as a banker, but that life had little attraction for him and he became a sailor. Macdonald's mixed heritage gave him an Asian look, which is perhaps why HBC boss George Simpson picked him in 1848 to infiltrate Japan, which was effectively closed to Europeans at the time.

Simpson had already expanded the HBC's trading empire into Alaska, thanks to a treaty with the Russians (who had not yet sold the territory to the United States), and down the Pacific Coast to San Francisco, which was part of Mexico. (When war broke out between Britain and Russia in 1854, the HBC had enough political muscle to ensure there was no fighting in Alaska.)

After the Americans provoked a war with Mexico in 1846 and effectively annexed California, Simpson closed down the San Francisco operation. By then he'd opened a trading post in Hawaii, which was still an independent kingdom. It was from Hawaii that Simpson sent Macdonald to Japan to gauge the level of U.S. influence there and to investigate the possibility of the HBC setting up operations.

On Simpson's instructions, Macdonald joined the whaler *Plymouth* in Hawaii and persuaded the captain to put him ashore near Hokkaido. There he told the local warlord that he was a shipwrecked sailor. He was sent as a prisoner to Nagasaki, which was the only place in Japan where Europeans were permitted. The Dutch trading post at Nagasaki was strictly supervised by the Japanese.

Macdonald was forced to teach 14 Japanese men how to speak English. Up until then, the Japanese had been trying to learn English from the Dutch traders. Macdonald's students, particularly Enosuke Moriyama, later became key participants when Japan negotiated trade treaties with America and Britain. (The British delegation was led by former Canadian governor general Lord Elgin.)

Macdonald spent almost a year as a prisoner of the Japanese. In 1849, he was released and turned over to the captain of an American warship that had been sent to collect 14 deserters who had also been captured by the Japanese authorities and were being held on a whaling ship.

The Scot eventually returned to Canada, where his family was living in the St. Andrews area of Québec, but his restless nature soon took him to what would shortly become British Columbia. There he ran a packing business, moving supplies to the gold miners on the Fraser River and the Cariboo fields. In 1864, he helped explore Vancouver Island and then returned to the area where he had been born, which was now U.S. territory.

Macdonald's contribution to opening Japan to the world wasn't appreciated at the time in Canada, and his book about the year he spent there, *A Canadian in Japan*, was not published until almost 30 years after his death in 1894. There are two monuments to Macdonald in Japan, one at Rishiri and the other at Nagasaki.

Chapter Four

How the Scots Saved Canada—Twice

Without the Highland Clearances in Scotland, Canada would be part of the United States. The role played by Scots, particularly Highland Scots, in repelling American invasions in 1775 and 1812 is overlooked these days. And many of those Scots would not have been in Canada if they hadn't been pushed out of their own country when their clan chiefs transformed into grasping landlords.

Scots had been making their way to the English colonies on the eastern seaboard of North America from the earliest days of settlement, but they tended to immigrate individually rather than in groups. That changed after the last Jacobite rebellion was ruthlessly crushed at the Battle of Culloden in 1746 and the British government decided to smash the clan system. The clan chiefs were reduced to mere landlords, whose prestige now depended more on rent income than on the number of fighting men they could muster. The chiefs decided the Scottish Highlands would produce more rent if people were replaced by sheep, and Highlanders were soon crossing the Atlantic in clan groups and settling together in New York state, Georgia and the Carolinas.

The 1763 Treaty of Paris opened the gates to major Scottish settlement in Canada, but the wave of immigrants that was most important for the country's security came from the United States after the so-called American Revolution.

A word about the "Revolution." It was really the First American Civil War. About one-third of the population supported the power grab by the New England aristocracy, another third was against it, and the remaining third just wanted to be left alone. The American attitude of "if you're not with us, you're against us" existed even then, and many members of the neutral third were terrorized into supporting the revolution. Those who weren't terrorized soon recognized which side was most likely to win after the British made a number of incredibly stupid military and political blunders.

The bulk of the recently arrived Highlanders supported the losing side in the revolution. They might have fought against King George II at Culloden, but they had been fighting to put another king on the throne. Despite the treatment they received at the hands of the British and their own chiefs, the Highlanders remained strong believers in the existing social order. Even Highland heroine Flora MacDonald, who had spent time in the Tower of London for helping Jacobite leader Bonnie Prince Charlie escape to France, rallied her fellow clansmen to the British side in North Carolina. An army of Highlanders attempted to join a British army sent to capture Charleston but were defeated by rebels at Moore's Creek. Some of the Highlanders, including MacDonald's husband Allan, eventually made it to Canada, where they continued their fight.

The final defeat of the French in Canada, recognized in the 1763 Treaty of Paris, was one of the main causes of the revolution. When the French and their Aboriginal allies threatened New England, the Yankee merchants were happy to have British troops to protect them. Once the French were gone, however, the New England aristocracy had its own plans for North America, which didn't include paying for British soldiers.

The first military governor of Québec, Scottish brigadier James Murray, warned of trouble early on. "If we are wise, we would return Canada to France," he wrote. "New England needs something to rub against."

The British authorities might have been more worried if they had realized the extent to which Yankee businessmen, including future president George Washington, were selling white settlers land that British treaties had promised to the Natives. The only thing that would keep Washington and his cronies out of jail for fraud was a government that refused to honour treaties made with the Natives.

There were many people in both New England and what became known as British North America who saw the rebellion as nothing more than a ruthless grab for control of the continent by a small clique of businessmen, and when the Yankee rebels invaded Québec, no one—apart from a handful of disgruntled, and misguided, Canadiens—welcomed them. However, active support for the British was lukewarm, and it was left to the Scots to put the muscle into resisting the rebel invasion.

A Scottish regiment known as the Cameronians garrisoned Montréal. The regiment traced its roots to the armed men who stood guard outside illegal Presbyterian prayer meetings on the windswept moors of the Scottish Lowlands in the mid to late 1600s. After Presbyterianism became legal again in 1688, the men were formed into a regular British Army regiment. They were sent to Canada in 1775 and garrisoned Montréal, Trois-Rivières, Chambly, Fort St. John (now St-Jean-Sur-Richelieu), Crown Point and Ticonderoga. Almost 10 years of garrison duty in North America had taken its toll on the regiment, which was under-strength and poorly led. As a result, it gave up Fort St. John and Chambly to General Richard Montgomery's rebel invasion force without a fight, and the British were soon retreating to Québec City.

The defence of Canada now depended on veterans of the war that had finally wrested control of the country from the French only a dozen years before. After the Treaty of Paris the British government gave free land to soldiers willing to settle in North America. The aim was to create a pool of loyal subjects with military experience in case further trouble arose. Many soldiers from the three Highland regiments that had fought the French in Canada—the Black Watch, the Montgomerie Highlanders and the Fraser Highlanders—grabbed the offer of free land with both hands. They settled mainly in Nova Scotia, on Prince Edward Island, along the St. Lawrence and in upper New York state.

The American invasion meant they were now expected to keep their part of the bargain and defend their new homeland. Former members of the three Highland regiments, and some of their older sons, were soon making their way to Québec City to join a new regiment called the Royal Highland Emigrants. They were issued uniforms that were a carbon copy of those worn by the regular Highland regiments of the British Army.

By the time two groups of Americans, led by Benedict Arnold and Richard Montgomery, began to close in on the city, about 200 Highlanders had gathered there. It wasn't many, but it was enough. The Highlanders under the command of Allan MacLean, a professional soldier and former Jacobite rebel, formed the shock troops for the British defence of the city. MacLean and his men arrived just in time to prevent a group of faint-hearted citizens from surrendering the city to Arnold.

Although General Guy Carleton officially commanded the garrison of Québec, he trusted MacLean to organize the defence. James Thompson, a veteran of the Fraser Highlanders who had fought against Montcalm's troops on the Plains of Abraham, was put in charge of building new defensive positions.

On the night of December 31, 1775, in the midst of a snowstorm, Captain Malcolm Fraser of the Royal Highland Emigrants spotted the signals that marked the first major rebel assault on the city. The Highlanders unleashed a devastating volley of musket fire that killed General Richard Montgomery and drove back the first assault. Several Highlanders who had chosen to fight for the rebels were among the 100 men killed in the attacks on Québec City.

The siege continued, but it was abandoned when a relief fleet carrying fresh British troops, including the Royal Scots Fusiliers, arrived. The Royal Highland Emigrants soon grew to form two battalions. The First Battalion took men from New York, Québec and Ontario.

The Second Battalion recruited volunteers drawn from Prince Edward Island, Nova Scotia and the Carolinas. In 1779, the regiment became an official part of the British Army, the 84th Foot, and its members fought in most of the major British campaigns of the revolution. When the regiment was disbanded, the Second Battalion men were given land in the Douglas area of Nova Scotia, while the First Battalion settled in the Stormont, Dundas and Glengarry areas of Ontario.

Nova Scotia had remained pretty much neutral in the war. Although the majority of its population was born in New England, the province lacked the established merchant aristocracy that led the rebellion in the 13 colonies. And the presence of the first waves of Highland immigrants provided a core of soldierly citizens firmly opposed to the rebels.

Glengarry, in Ontario, was to prove one of the most important areas of Canada for later military recruitment. The story of Highland settlement there goes back to 1773, when three brothers from Glengarry, Scotland, led 400 of their clansmen to New York state. The brothers, Allan, Alexander and John Macdonnell, and their followers were welcomed to the Mohawk Valley by the uncrowned king of the area, Irishman William Johnson. The first Macdonnell settlers were soon joined in Tyron County by others from the western Scottish Highlands north of Fort William.

The Glengarry men came down firmly on the Loyalist side when the revolution broke out, especially when five of their leaders were taken hostage by rebel general Philip Schuyler. Scots were soon involved in some of the bitterest fighting of the whole war. The Yankees and the recent German settlers who were their allies accused the Loyalists of beginning the cycle of atrocity and counter-atrocity that marked the fighting in the Mohawk and Hudson valleys. Of course, the Loyalists accused the rebels of starting the cycle that saw civilians burned to death and tortured. The presence of Native people on the Loyalist side infuriated the rebels, and no fewer than 40 Aboriginal towns were torched. Leather made from the flayed bodies of the dead became popular souvenirs of the fighting.

For centuries, Highland society had been fine-tuned for war. Social standing denoted military rank, with the chiefs becoming regimental colonels in time of war and their sons the majors. Captains and lieutenants were drawn from the middlemen of Highland society, the tacksmen, who held land in their own right and collected the chief's rents. The Macdonnell brothers were tacksmen, and the Glengarry men of Tyron County were nearly able to form a full-fledged military unit on their own. Most of them went into the King's Royal Regiment of New York. There were seven Macdonnells serving as officers, and a total of 22 men born in Scotland were in command positions.

After the rebels won the war, there was no question of the Glengarry men returning to what had now been named Montgomery County. Almost 1500 settled in the Glengarry, Stormont and Dundas areas of Ontario.

The King's Royal Regiment of New York and the Royal Highland Emigrants weren't the only Scottish regiments to fight against the rebels. Highlanders, possibly lured by promises of free land in North America after a British victory, flocked to join the kilted regiments being raised in Britain to fight the rebels, and it has been estimated that 60,000 Highlanders crossed the Atlantic with the British Army to fight in the American Revolution.

It's not surprising, then, that the Scots in general were no longer welcome in the new United States after the rebels won. The shorter their time in the country before the revolution, the less welcome they were, and most of the Highlanders were recent arrivals. When Thomas Jefferson was drawing up the Declaration of Independence, he nearly included a denunciation of the Scots. In 1782, Georgia passed a law forbidding Scots from settling or trading in the state unless they could prove their rebel credentials.

Highlanders formed the bulk of the estimated 40,000 United Empire Loyalists who made their homes in British North America following the war. Most went to New Brunswick or Nova Scotia, but 2000 opted for the relative wilds of Ontario. Of course, the success of the revolution didn't result in the wholesale expulsion of Scots from the new United States. The 1790 census conducted after the war's end found 8 percent of the population claimed Scottish heritage. And of the 56 signatures on the Declaration of Independence, 21 were of men who considered themselves at least partly Scottish—though only two were born in Scotland.

The expulsion of the United Empire Loyalists created a pool of Scots in Canada with a marked hatred for Yankees, and none were to prove more crucial to the survival of the country when the next invasion came than the Glengarry men.

As the tempo of evictions from Glengarry in Scotland increased, the original settlers in the Canadian Glengarry were joined by more and more of their friends and family from back home. The Macdonnell chiefs and their neighbours in Scotland were in the forefront of the move to rid the land of people and replace them with sheep. People in present-day Glengarry, Scotland, still talk of the day when a ship that was to pick up a group of evicted tenants at Loch Hourn failed to arrive. Instead of allowing the tenants to return to Glengarry to await a new ship, the landowner placed men with guns on the only pass that led from Loch Hourn with orders to shoot anyone who left the seashore. The huddled peasants were forced to live on seaweed until the replacement ship showed up. Loch Hourn's name was well earned—it means Hell Inlet.

The Glengarry Scots got a further boost in 1804 when a group of men of the disbanded Glengarry Fencibles, a British army regiment raised for home-defence duties only, arrived en masse with their families to settle. The regiment of displaced Catholic Highlanders, mainly Macdonnells, was accompanied to Canada by its founder, Father Alexander Macdonnell, who later became a Canadian bishop. The government gave the disbanded soldiers land in the Cornwall area. Another 1100 settlers arrived the same year from the western Highland mainland and the Isle of Skye.

By the time the Americans invaded during the War of 1812, there were an estimated 10,000 Highlanders living in Ontario. That figure did not include a British regiment of Highlanders raised specifically for service in Canada with promises of free land. Recruits to the Canadian Regiment of Fencibles were promised they could take their families with them when they travelled from Glasgow across the Atlantic. But when the time came to sail, the soldiers were told to leave their families behind and march to the Isle of Wight in southern England for shipment to Canada. The soldiers, many of them fathers and sons, believed they were being tricked into serving in India and refused to leave Glasgow. The men were eventually persuaded to march to Ayr, but by then the British government had had enough of them, and the regiment was disbanded. The government had been under pressure to disperse the regiment anyway by the landowners, who resented losing their tenants on anything but their own terms. Some of the mutineers were court-martialled, but the court was, by the standards of the time, lenient with the soldiers when they produced evidence of the exaggerated rewards, such as free cattle, promised to them by the regimental recruiters. One of the ringleaders was sentenced to 800 lashes; another got 500. Recruiters from other Highland regiments swooped down on Ayr and persuaded the youngest and fittest of the former Fencibles to join them. They were sent to fight in Egypt and Portugal, and few, if any, fulfilled their dream of a new life in Canada.

But the Highlanders who did make the crossing were to prove crucial in repelling the American invasion of Canada. As early as 1807, with tension growing in the wake of the U.S. government's open musings about expansion, there was talk of forming the Glengarry men into a defence force. Some had already briefly served with the Royal Canadian Volunteer Regiment of Foot, which had been formed in 1796 and disbanded in 1802. Ultimately, the Glengarry Regiment of Light Infantry Fencibles first paraded in May 1812. The formation of a regiment of expert backwoodsmen did not come a moment too soon. The first American invaders crossed the Detroit River in July.

On paper, the war should have been a walkover for the Americans. The regular British Army was locked in a war in Europe against the forces of French dictator Napoleon. The British had only 4500 regular troops in British North America, and many of them were assigned to protect the crucial timber supplies being cut in Atlantic Canada for the war effort. Only 1400 regulars were available for the defence of what was then called Upper Canada (now southern Ontario), and many of them were second-rate. The Americans had 5500 regulars (fortunately, many of them were third-rate) and 100,000 militia. The Canadian militia numbered just under 4000 at the time. Luckily, many of the militia were Scots.

The role of the militia in winning the War of 1812 has become exaggerated over the years, the result of the myth-mongering involved in nation building. But the militia did prevent defeat until the seasoned regulars of the British Army could arrive from Europe and force the Americans to accept the pre-war status quo.

The Scottish fur traders of the Montréal-based North West Company struck the first blow against the Americans. General Isaac Brock, the British commander in Upper Canada, enlisted the muscle of the company's men and their knowledge of the headwaters of the Mississippi to seize the U.S. fort on Mackinac Island in Lake Michigan. Its capture secured the west on both sides of the 49th parallel for the rest of the war and ensured the Canadian fur trade could continue unmolested. The North West Company formed its own militia regiment, the Corps des Voyageurs Canadiens, with the company's Scottish partners supplying the bulk of the officers and the tough Canadien coureurs de bois providing the foot soldiers.

After capturing Mackinac Island, Brock turned his attention to the American troops who had crossed the Detroit River with General William Hull on July 11. Two of the first men wounded in the American invasion were Scots officers serving with the 41st Foot,

Captain Muir and Lieutenant Sutherland. The faint-hearted Hull didn't stay long on Canadian soil. When he heard Brock was coming with a force made up of British regulars, militia and Natives, Hull retreated back to the U.S. fort at Detroit. Failing to realize the military superiority he actually had, he then surrendered the fort to Brock.

Scots played a prominent part in the Battle of Queenston Heights on October 13, 1812, in which Brock was killed. After Brock was shot as he led the first charge against the American invaders occupying the heights, Lieutenant Colonel John Macdonnell led the second charge. He too was shot and killed, but the charge he led kept the Americans pinned down while the reinforcements moved into the positions from which they swept the invaders back across the Detroit River. Macdonnell's fall was witnessed by his old friend Archibald McLean, who was serving as an officer in the York Volunteers, a unit from what is now Toronto, which contained many Scots. In July 1814, McLean was captured in the early stages of the bloody Battle of Lundy's Lane, but he survived the war to become chief justice of Ontario.

The victory at Queenston Heights also owed much to John Norton, a Métis brought up in Scotland. He led a force of Six Nations (Iroquois) warriors onto the heights via a devious route, which Brock might have been better to take, and launched a surprise attack that pinned the Americans down until British reinforcements could arrive.

Another Scot who played an important part in rallying the Native people to the British side was Robert Dickson, a red-headed and -bearded giant born in Dumfries. He married the daughter of a Sioux chief and worked as a fur trader west of the Mississippi. He led a group of 400 Natives who joined the small force of British regulars and North West Company men who captured Mackinac Island in the early days of the war. Dickson and his men are also credited with scaring General Hull into surrendering Detroit to Brock.

Dickson joined forces with the legendary Shawnee war chief Tecumseh for a time, and after Tecumseh's death, he participated in the capture of two American schooners off Mackinac Island. Toward the end of the war, he was criticized for favouring the Sioux too much and lost much of his influence.

Meanwhile, as the tempo of the war increased, so did the involvement of the men from Glengarry and the surrounding communities. The Glengarry Fencibles were kitted out in a dark green uniform similar to the one worn by the elite troops of the British Army's Rifle Brigade. Their skill in the arts of camouflage earned them the nickname "The Black Stump Brigade" from their Native allies, who were impressed by the Scots' ability to merge into the bush. The fencibles were even called on to train newly arrived British regulars from the Warwickshire Regiment and the Prince of Wales's Volunteers in the art of bush fighting.

When news arrived in October 1813 that an American army was heading for Montréal, around 600 Glengarry men covered 170 miles in less than three days to confront it at the Chateauguay River. The fencibles under the command of "Red George" Macdonnell joined a larger force of Canadien militia under the command of Lieutenant Colonel Charles de Salaberry to repulse an American army that was six times larger. Earlier that year, Red George (who was born in Newfoundland) and his Glengarries had captured Ogdensburg in an unauthorized attack across the icebound St. Lawrence River that took the Americans completely by surprise.

As well as providing a regiment of fencibles, who were treated as regular soldiers but who could not be sent overseas, the Glengarry area supplied two militia battalions for the defence of Upper Canada. Their mainly Highland neighbours in Stormont and Dundas counties each raised one militia battalion. Scots were prominent in most militia units, including one sent from Nova Scotia. The First Battalion of Embodied Militia even chose a thistle for the crest on its regimental belt.

One of the British regiments that had been in Canada since the start of the war was the Royal Scots. It recruited heavily while in Québec, and by the time of the invasion it had a large number of Canadiens and Irish immigrants in its ranks. It was ironic that the regiment took on such a French character, because before entering British service it had been a Scottish mercenary regiment in the French army. The Royal Scots were involved in several battles of the war and lost 172 men at the slog-fest known as the Battle of Lundy's Lane (more on Lundy's Lane later).

Other Scottish units of the British Army that fought in the war included the 70th Glasgow Lowland Regiment (which in a bizarre twist became part of the East Surrey Regiment in 1820) and the 90th Perthshire Volunteers, a unit reputedly recruited from the jails of Scotland. The Royal Scots Fusiliers were part of the British force that, in August 1814, took the war to Washington and burned the presidential mansion, which became known as the White House because of the whitewash used to hide the scorch marks after the war. The Fusiliers even dined on a banquet that had been prepared for the U.S. president, James Madison, to celebrate the expected American victory in the battle for the capital.

Armies can't fight without bullets and bread, but the men who get these essentials into the hands of the soldiers are often forgotten. It is no surprise, then, that Scots-born Robert Nichol is seldom mentioned as a leading figure in the War of 1812. Nichol was already a successful businessman, having come to Canada to work as a seaman on the Great Lakes freighters, when he donned the uniform of the Norfolk Militia. Even though the Americans had seized eight of his trading ships in 1808, he had to be persuaded by Brock to join the war effort. Nichol soon found himself organizing the transport of British troops around Upper Canada and supplying them with food and ammunition. But Nichol was no deskbound warrior. As well as masterminding the Canadian military supply organization, he fought in several battles and had at least one horse shot out from under him. The Americans burned his home and milling businesses to the ground in retaliation for the role he was playing in their defeat. Another Scot, James Macaulay, set up the military hospitals that treated soldiers wounded in the war.

The two generals who followed Brock as commanders in Upper Canada, Roger Sheaffe and Francis de Rottenburg, proved timid and uninspired. It took a Scot, General Gordon Drummond, to put some fire back into the war against the invaders. Drummond was born in Québec, where his father was a prominent merchant and civil servant. However, when Drummond was four years old his father died, and his family returned to the ancestral mansion in Perthshire, Scotland. He was educated in Britain, joined the army as an officer as soon as he was old enough, and served in Canada for four years before he was posted to Ireland shortly before the American invasion. He arrived back in Canada in late 1813 to find the Americans firmly entrenched in southwestern Ontario. In a brilliant lightning campaign, Drummond drove the Americans back across the Niagara frontier and restored confidence in the British, which had been withering until then.

Drummond's star faded a little after the Battle of Lundy's Lane, where British and American forces collided almost by accident and became caught up in a point-blank shootout involving musket volleys and cannons. By the end of the day, both sides had suffered 850 casualties. The British occupied Lundy's Lane itself, but historians now agree the Americans won the fight and then staged a strategic withdrawal. It is also said that the Americans took advantage of the very short range at which the battle was fought to load their muskets with three balls at a time.

Drummond was wounded in the neck at Lundy's Lane, which may explain his poor performance in one of the last major battles of the war at Fort Erie. His plan to recapture the fort from the Americans was too complicated and was wrecked when an ammunition dump at the fort suddenly exploded and killed most of the assault soldiers who had managed to get inside.

The Americans abandoned the fort and retreated soon after because of supply shortages. American support for the war was fading as the Royal Navy, freed from its duties in Europe following the defeat of Napoleon, took the offensive along the Atlantic seaboard.

The failed attack on Fort Erie involved the Royal Scots and some of the Glengarry men. Both units are

now history, but their successors—the First Battalion
of the Royal Regiment of Scotland in the case of the
Royal Scots, and the reservists of the Stormont, Dundas and Glengarry Highlanders—share the battle
honour "Niagara" in memory of the part they played in
the War of 1812.

The present-day Glengarries go even further in
maintaining their link with the Highlanders who twice
saved Canada by claiming regimental descent from
the Royal Highland Emigrants, the King's Royal Regiment of New York and the Glengarry fencibles.

CULLODEN AND THE HIGHLAND CLEARANCES

The Battle of Culloden in 1746 did not cause the Highland Clearances in Scotland. The old, semi-feudal society
of the Highlands was bound to change as the economic
realities of the Industrial Revolution made themselves
felt. What Culloden did was speed up the process.

The Highlands and Islands had long been a problem
for the British authorities. Their inhabitants spoke Gaelic,
not English, and belonged to a society structured more
for war than wage-slavery. The partnership between
landed interests and the growing merchant classes in
England and Glasgow that ran Britain was looking for an
excuse to destroy Gaelic culture, and the Jacobite rebellion of 1745 gave them one.

Contrary to what most people believe these days,
there were more Highlanders fighting on the British government's side than with the rebels. Out of 32,000 available swordsmen in the Highlands and Islands, fewer
than 4000 rallied to the Jacobite cause in an attempt to
restore the exiled Stuart family to the British throne. But
it was the fourth time Highlanders had joined Jacobite

rebellion, and that was excuse enough. After the mainly Highland rebel army was defeated by British troops on Culloden Moor, near Inverness, the sins of those 4000 were visited on the entire Highlands. British troops spread out across the western Highlands, burning and pillaging regardless of which side clans had been on in the rebellion.

It became a crime to wear a kilt or carry a weapon of any kind, even a knife. The clan chiefs were transformed from community leaders, who their people believed held the land in trust for the benefit of all, into landowners whose sole interest was maximum profit—and sheep proved more profitable per acre than human beings. The process started before 1745, and disgruntled Highlanders had begun settling in North Carolina in the 1730s, but what began as a trickle became a torrent in the aftermath of Culloden. Landlords evicted their tenants without cause or raised the rents until no one could afford them. Some cared nothing for where their clansmen went; others organized or subsidized passage to Canada. The landlords could afford to help their tenants a little because the evictions increased their income tenfold. Soon the only sound heard in Highland glens that once echoed with children's laughter was the bleating of sheep.

But it didn't always suit the clan chiefs to see people leave. There was good money to be had in selling young male tenants en masse as regiments for the British Army. And few of the tenants, who came from generations of warriors loyal only to their chief, challenged the landlord's right to do this. In any case, the alternative was the eviction of their parents from their homes. As late as the 1790s, the landlords' recruiters paraded the able-bodied young men of a neighbourhood and indicated the ones destined for the British Army by offering them a pinch of snuff.

The landlords also had business ventures, such as fishing or harvesting seaweed to be turned into industrial alkali, that required a pool of cheap labour. They came up with the crofting system, which gave each family just enough land to grow potatoes and avoid starvation but did not provide enough money to allow the men to refuse to work for the landlord. When the landlords' schemes went bust, people were left on the poverty line. Crofters were never intended to make a living from their land, and the crofts got smaller as they were subdivided over the years among sons and then grandsons.

In 1803, the Highland Society, which represented the interests of the chiefs and other major landowners, persuaded the British government to pass an Act of Parliament ensuring better safety on the emigrant ships. They claimed to be acting for humanitarian reasons, but they knew that the act would triple the price of a ticket to Canada and put it out of reach for many of their tenants.

Faced with a choice between life in the Highlands, where the dice were loaded in the landlord's favour, and the promise of free land in Canada surrounded by fellow Gaelic speakers, it's not surprising so many opted to cross the Atlantic. Certainly the descendants of the Highlanders who came to Canada enjoy a higher standard of living than the descendants of those who stayed behind or migrated to the slums of Glasgow and the surrounding areas, and many present-day residents of the Highlands and Islands would rather be living in Canada.

Between 1746 and 1815, about 15,000 Highlanders came over from Scotland to Canada, but the loss to the

Highlands and Islands should not be measured in numbers of people who crossed the Atlantic, but in the quality of those who left. It was the brightest and bravest who made the passage in the great sailing ships.

Canada's First Spymaster

The French Revolution in 1793 made Scots fur trader John Richardson one of Canada's first spymasters.

The Aberdeenshire man was no stranger to danger. During the American Revolution, he had served on an armed merchant ship that was given official permission to intercept rebel ships and confiscate their cargoes. Privateering, as it was known, could be a profitable business. Unfortunately, Richardson's ship, the *Vengeance*, was attacked by a Royal Navy warship, which loosed five or six broadsides into it before sailing off without an apology.

Richardson returned to the Montréal-based fur trade in 1782 and teamed up with other Scots to form the North West Company, which was all too often a deadly rival of the Hudson's Bay Company until 1821. In 1792, he won election to the Lower Canada House of Assembly as a representative for Montréal East.

Richardson believed that French revolutionaries and their American allies inspired the 1796 riots in Montréal against a law that forced people to work on the roads in their free time. Other leading politicians in the province agreed, and Richardson was appointed to sniff out the foreign spies and their collaborators in Canada.

Richardson discovered that the French ambassador in Washington was sending agents across the border into Canada to recruit Canadiens to help storm the British garrison at Québec City when a French invasion force arrived in the St. Lawrence from its base in the Caribbean. He arrested three suspects, but they were later cleared. Fellow Scot John McLane was not so lucky. He had a timber business based in Rhode Island and claimed to be looking for suppliers in Canada when he was arrested. McLane was fingered by yet another Scot, John Black, as a "French general" who had tried to enlist Black in the plot to capture Québec City. Black was a British spy who spent years building a reputation as a radical republican friend of the French. McLane was convicted of treason, beheaded and disembowelled.

Richardson next foiled the plot of Vermont adventurers, led by Ira Allen, who planned to invade Canada with the help of a secret society Allen had established in Montréal. The Scot arrested the secret society's leaders.

The threat of a French-sponsored American invasion of Canada seemed to soar when Jérôme Bonaparte, brother of French dictator Napoleon, turned up in Washington in 1803. An army of informers was sent into towns on both sides of the border to look for signs of trouble. Richardson's greatest coup was turning Canadien traitor Jacques Rousse into a double agent for the British and foiling the French invasion plan in its infancy. The Scot believed that secret clauses in the Louisiana Purchase treaty of 1803, in which the French sold Louisiana to the Americans, included a guarantee to support a United States invasion of Canada.

Richardson was also involved in an 1807 scheme to persuade the New England states to break away from their expansionist western cousins in the event of an American invasion of Canada. The scheme almost backfired when John Henry, the Irishman sent to stir up the New Englanders, decided he had been given a raw deal by the British and sold his secret instructions to the Americans. The sale fuelled the Americans' suspicions of the British, but when the Americans fulfilled Richardson's predictions and invaded Canada in 1812, New Englanders' support of the war was at best lukewarm.

The John Henry incident marked the end of Richardson's days as a spymaster and he returned to the fur trade, which made him a very rich man.

JOHN NORTON

John Norton was the son of a Cherokee man who had been captured as a child and taken to Britain. The captive, known to history only as Norton, married a Scotswoman called Anderson. Their son John was probably born in Dunfermline in Fife. The elder Norton ran a printshop in the Scottish town.

John, like many young Scots at the time, received a good education and came to Canada in 1785 as a private in the British Army. He deserted in 1787 and he was formally discharged from the army in 1788. Norton then worked as a teacher at a Mohawk settlement on the Bay of Quinte for three years before going into the fur trade.

It wasn't long before John Norton was working as personal interpreter for the legendary Chief Joseph Brant of the Six Nations. Norton found himself heavily involved in Native land claims directed at the British government and was sent by Brant on a secret mission to England with the aim of gaining permission to sell Native land to white settlers. Brant's initiative was controversial among the people of the Six Nations, and Norton's mission was a failure. Norton returned to Canada but, fed up with personal attacks on him by members of the Six Nations, headed south to Tennessee to explore his Cherokee heritage.

He returned to Canada in time to rally Native support for the British in anticipation of an American invasion. When the Americans finally invaded in 1812, Norton led a band of warriors that fought in several of the major battles of the war, including Queenston Heights, Chippawa and Lundy's Lane. His role in the war earned him a pension of £200 a year, but he spent years fighting the British to get better treatment for the Aboriginal veterans of the conflict.

In 1813, at the age of 50, he married a 16-year-old girl from the Delaware tribe. After a short stay in Scotland, the couple farmed near present-day Brantford. The age difference may have been too much, because in 1823, Norton fought a duel with a man he believed to be his wife's lover. Norton killed the man. He was found guilty of manslaughter, paid his fine and vanished.

THE LADIES FROM HELL

The skirl of pipes sounds in the cool, crisp, Afghan morning. The Canadian army doesn't have any pipers on the payroll officially, but even in dusty Kandahar, soldiers pay tribute to the military's Scottish heritage. On most missions in the past few decades, at least two or three soldiers have brought their bagpipes. There was a reason that the pipes were once banned as a weapon of war by a British government bent on destroying the military potential of the Scots Highlanders.

Highland soldiers played an important role in repelling American invasions of Canada in 1775 and 1812, and the traditionally warlike, and Tory, Highlanders turned out in force to repulse an unofficial American invasion in 1837 in support of William Lyon Mackenzie's revolutionaries.

No fewer than four militia regiments were raised in the Glengarry area at that time.

Highland regiments from the British Army often did garrison duty in Canada, and there were frequent disputes over their kilts' suitability for the winter climate. When the British began withdrawing their garrisons from Canada, the militia units that were left to hold the still-expansionist Americans at bay were reluctant to don kilts. In 1857, there were Highland militia companies, several of them clad in tartan trews, in Montréal, London, Toronto, Hamilton and Kingston.

By the 1870s, only two militia battalions—the 94th Victoria Highland Provisional Battalion and the 79th Colchester and Hants, both from Nova Scotia—were promoting a definite Scottish identity. But many militia units were attracting large numbers of Scots, no doubt driven by their homeland's military traditions. The Scots always prided themselves on being warriors who were fierce as lions in battle and gentle as lambs in peacetime. The growing repute of the British Army's Highland regiments, fanned by jingoistic newspaper reports across the Empire, made all things Scottish popular. As a result, militia units were soon seeking Scottish identities.

Montréal, home to many of the Scots business tycoons who pulled the financial and political strings in the years around Confederation, was one of the first cities to have a militia unit with a definite Scottish identity when the 5th Battalion Royal Light Infantry morphed into the Royal Scots Fusiliers in 1880, then the Royal Scots of Canada four years later, and finally the Royal Highlanders of Canada. The regiment modelled itself on the British Army's Black Watch, and it officially became the Black Watch of Canada in 1920.

When the 48th Highlanders was formed in Toronto in 1891, it took on a Scottish identity that has survived to this day. In the run-up to World War I, several new militia regiments were formed, many of which adopted Highland identities. Often the regimental numbers assigned to them mirrored the numbers associated with the British Army's Highland regiments. When Hamilton's 91st Highlanders was formed in 1903, for example, the number was a tribute to Scotland's Argyll and Sutherland Highlanders. The Argyll and Sutherland Highlanders of Canada are still based in Hamilton. Similarly, the Winnipeg-based Queen's Own Cameron Highlanders of Canada snagged the same 79th label as the Camerons in Britain, and the Seaforths in Vancouver shared the 72nd number with their British cousins.

The outbreak of the First World War brought men flocking to fight the "beastly Hun" on the battlefields of northwest Europe. Canadian militia minister Sam Hughes decided not to send existing militia units but to form composite battalions. This didn't work out as planned, though, because whole militia regiments volunteered en masse. Among the very first Canadian troops to arrive in Europe were the kilted soldiers of the 1st Canadian Division's 3rd Brigade, which was made up of the Canadian Expeditionary Force's 13th Battalion, 15th Battalion and 16th Battalion. The 13th Battalion was really the Black Watch from Montréal, the 15th was drawn from Toronto's 48th Highlanders, and the 16th Battalion was a composite unit drawn from Vancouver's Seaforths, Winnipeg's Camerons, Hamilton's Argylls and Victoria's Gordons. The first Canadian contingent included many ex-servicemen, and no fewer than 850 men with the 16th Battalion had seen previous service with the British

Army. There were also soldiers who had fought as mercenaries in China and with the French Foreign Legion.

The 3rd Brigade was key in foiling a German attack at Pyres in 1915 that threatened to smash through the British trench positions after neighbouring French troops fled in the face of the war's first poison gas attack. Lance Corporal Frederick Fisher of the 13th Battalion became Canada's first winner of the Victoria Cross, the top gallantry award in the British Empire, for his work repelling the Germans. The machine gunner was killed during the fighting, but the medal was presented to his family.

The Highlanders of the 3rd Brigade were joined by other Canadian units with a distinctly Scottish flavour, including the Highland Light Infantry of Canada, the Nova Scotia Highlanders, the Seaforth Highlanders and the Cameron Highlanders. Montréal's Black Watch also managed to muster two more battalions to join the 13th Battalion. The Canadian Corps soon earned the reputation for providing the best assault troops on the Western Front, and the man who commanded them was Arthur Currie, former commander of Victoria's Gordon Highlanders of Canada. The British provided the corps with a number of experienced officers, and serving with the Canadians marked several of them for greatness. No fewer than three of those officers rose to be supreme commander of the British Army during World War II.

The ferocity of kilted Highlanders on the battlefield earned them the nickname "the Ladies from Hell," and by the end of the war, even more Canadian regiments wanted to be Scottish. In 1922, the Ottawa Regiment become the Ottawa Highlanders. The Essex Fusiliers became the Essex Scottish in 1927, and the Lorne Scots got their name in 1936. In 1921, the Calgary Regiment donned the kilt, but it did not become the Calgary

Highlanders until 1928. The Stormont, Dundas and Glengarry Highlanders, who claimed descent from the men who beat off the Americans in 1812, donned the kilt in 1922. After the Second World War, yet another unit, the Lake Superior Regiment, took on a Scottish identity and became the Lake Superior Scottish.

During World War II, Canadian Scottish regiments were in the forefront of the fighting. The Essex Scottish and Winnipeg's Queen's Own Cameron Highlanders of Canada were at Dieppe. Among the first Canadians to land on D-Day in 1944 were the Cameron Highlanders of Ottawa; the Canadian Scottish; the Highland Light Infantry of Canada; the Stormont, Dundas and Glengarry Highlanders; and the Nova Scotia Highlanders. The Black Watch was reduced to just 15 men following a disastrous attempt to break out of the Normandy beachhead. The first Canadians across the Rhine, if you don't count the 1st Canadian Parachute Battalion, were the Highland Light Infantry of Canada.

The respect for education that Canadians inherited from the Scots meant they made up a large part of British Bomber Command during the Second World War. Aircrew from the Commonwealth and Scotland provided the backbone of Bomber Command in the form of navigators, radio operators and flight engineers.

For the final push on Germany, the 1st Canadian Army was joined by the veteran 1st Canadian Division, including the Seaforths and the 48th Highlanders, which had been fighting hard in Italy since 1943. Until the 1st Division arrived from Italy, Britain had lent Scottish troops to the 1st Canadian Army to bring it up to strength. All three of the Scottish infantry divisions—the 15th Scottish, the 51st Highland and the 52nd Lowland—served with the 1st Canadian Army between D-Day and Germany's surrender.

After the war ended, defence cuts meant proud Scottish regiments, such as the Cape Breton Highlanders, the Perth Regiment and the Scots Fusiliers, disappeared from the army list. All the Canadian Scottish units are now part of the reserve, though the Black Watch was a full-time regular army unit between 1953 and 1969. Many of the Scot-based reserve units have pipe bands composed of part-time soldiers and civilian musicians. Even some of the non-Scottish-affiliated battalions, such as the Loyal Edmonton Regiment, have pipe bands. The air force has a pipe band and its own tartan. The Lanark and Renfrew Scottish is part of the Royal Canadian Artillery in an air-defence role.

The Scottish tradition continues to run strong in the Canadian army, with 15 of the 47 reserve infantry battalions claiming affiliation with Auld Scotia. The battalions now contain people from various ethnic backgrounds, but somehow they all look good in kilts, just as they did in the early days of the Canadian army, when the ethnic diversity of the Canadian kilted troops was the subject of much comment during World War I.

Scottish Canadian Units

The Black Watch (Royal Highland Regiment) of
Canada (Montréal)

The Royal Highland Fusiliers of Canada (Cambridge)

The Lorne Scots (Peel Dufferin and Halton Regiment)
(Brampton)

The Stormont, Dundas and Glengarry Highlanders
(Cornwall)

The Nova Scotia Highlanders (Truro/Sydney)

The Essex Scottish (Windsor)

The Cameron Highlanders of Ottawa (Ottawa)

The 48th Highlanders of Canada (Toronto)

The Argyll and Sutherland Highlanders of Canada
(Princess Louise's) (Hamilton)

The Lake Superior Scottish Regiment (Thunder Bay)

The Queen's Own Cameron Highlanders of Canada
(Winnipeg)

The Calgary Highlanders (Calgary)

The Seaforth Highlanders of Canada (Vancouver)

The Canadian Scottish Regiment (Princess Mary's)
(Vancouver Island)

The Toronto Scottish (Queen Elizabeth the Queen
Mother's Own) (Toronto)

CHAPTER FIVE

THE SCOTS EXPLORE CANADA

Dreams of a practical route from the Atlantic to the Pacific and the riches of the Orient beyond drove Scots explorers to cross the Rockies and seek the outlets of western rivers. Strangely enough, the first major attempt to reach the Pacific by land ended up in the ice-bound channels of the Arctic.

Alexander Mackenzie, a Scot from the Isle of Lewis, was acting on bad information from a very bad man. Mackenzie was a fur trader with the North West Company when he set out for the Pacific in 1789, but a few years earlier he had been with a rival outfit, Gregory, McLeod and Co., which was locked in a bitter and often bloody battle with the Nor'Westers for control of the fur-rich Athabasca country. In 1787, when John Ross, one of Gregory, McLeod and Co.'s leading fur traders, was murdered by a Nor'Wester, Mackenzie took word of Ross's death to Montréal. The outfit quickly agreed to a merger with the North West Company. Mackenzie found himself working for Yankee fur trader Peter Pond, the main suspect in Ross's murder. Pond was a nasty piece of work who had allegedly killed at least one other rival trader in the past.

Based on information from local Natives, Pond had come to believe that a river emerging from the west end of Great Slave Lake led to the Pacific. His belief infected the highly ambitious Mackenzie, who set out from Fort Chipewyan on June 3, 1789, with three canoes manned by five voyageurs and six Natives. The handsome 25-year-old was a driven man. He would need all his grit and determination for the journey ahead.

One of the canoes was wrecked in rapids on the Slave River before the expedition even reached Great Slave Lake, and it took two more weeks of probing along the lake's ice-bound shores to find the river leading west. When they finally located the river, it looked wide and promising as a trade route. But as the Rockies came into dim view on the far horizon, the river turned northward.

Mackenzie pushed his voyageurs hard. They began paddling around 3 AM, and the fiery, moody Scot kept them at it until 9 PM. Mackenzie kept hoping the river would swing west and take him through the Rockies, but on July 10, the two canoes reached the maze of low-lying islands that marked its end. Beyond the river mouth was pack ice. The river was not the dreamed-of trade artery to the Orient, and Mackenzie named it "River of Disappointment." After a few days of measuring tidal flow and taking navigational readings, he set off on the return journey to Fort Chipewyan. Against the flow of the river the paddlers could make only 30 miles a day, instead of the 100 they managed on their way north. The expedition returned to the trading post at Fort Chipewyan 102 days after it left. The 2060-mile waterway Mackenzie travelled was soon renamed in his honour.

But all was not lost. On the journey back up the River of Disappointment, Mackenzie heard stories from the Natives about a river just west of the mountains that did lead to the Pacific. Mackenzie vowed to try again and to be better prepared in the future. He blamed his failure, in part, on his lack of skill in calculating navigational longitude correctly. He therefore travelled to London, where he studied astronomy and navigation. By September 1792, he was ready to try again.

Mackenzie realized he would almost certainly be unable to reach the Pacific and return in one summer season, so he decided to spend the winter at the junction of the Peace and Smoky rivers. The push for the Pacific began on May 9, 1793. Mackenzie, his trusty Scots lieutenant Alexander McKay (who would be speared to death in the waters of Clayoquot Sound 18 years later when Natives attacked a ship belonging to the American-owned Pacific Fur Company) and his crew of eight, plus a dog, set out in a 25-foot canoe in a bid to be the first men to cross the continent north of the Mexican border.

On May 17, sooner than Mackenzie expected, the glistening snow-capped peaks of the Rockies came into clear view. But before they could reach the mountains, he and his men spent a week battling the raging waters of the Peace River Canyon. The voyageurs feared they were signing their own death warrants unless they turned back, but Mackenzie bullied and bribed them to complete the 20-mile journey through the canyon. The worst part was a nine-mile portage that took four days. Eventually the river widened again and slowed down.

The canoe emerged on May 31 from a gloomy forest of jackpine and spruce onto the wide water that marks the junction of the Parsnip and Finlay rivers. Mackenzie was faced with the choice of following the Finlay north or going south on the Parsnip. He chose correctly and headed south. Local Natives had told him that the Parsnip would take him toward the "stinking waters" where white men travelled in canoes the size of islands with sails as big as clouds.

The Parsnip led to the Continental Divide, and a portage of 817 paces, stepped out by Mackenzie himself, put the canoe in what was dubbed the Bad River (now known as James Creek). It was well named. Within a few miles the bucking rapids had swamped the canoe and torn its bottom out. The explorers clung for their lives to the wreckage and were carried downstream by the raging waters before finally coming to rest against a sandbar. Once again the voyageurs were for turning back, but Mackenzie sat down and doggedly began repairing the canoe on his own. His show of determination shamed the paddle men into going on.

By June 17, they had left the Bad River and were travelling down a waterway that Mackenzie was calling the Grand River. The canoe was swept up into a wide current that carried them north briefly before turning south again. Some Aboriginal men on the bank shot at the canoe, but their arrows dropped well short. Farther along, the canoe was attacked again. This time Mackenzie turned for shore. After stuffing several pistols in his belt and grabbing some mirrors and beads as gifts, Mackenzie walked up to the men. They told him he would not be able to get much farther down the river because a series of rapids and water-falls hemmed in by deep canyons made the waterway impassable to canoes. After listening to the Native men, Mackenzie decided to abandon the Grand River and strike west on foot.

The party set out on July 4 along a trail that was well used by the local Carrier people. The voyageurs each carried 90 pounds of provisions on their backs while Mackenzie and McKay managed 70 pounds. The two Natives in the group at first refused to carry any packs at all, but were eventually persuaded to haul 45 pounds each. The ten men were soon encountering Native people who had trade goods that could only have come from Europeans or Americans. One child was wearing an earring made from a 1787 coin minted in Massachusetts.

Two weeks of marching through the dank forest and pouring Pacific rain brought Mackenzie's party to Bella Coola, where they managed to hire a couple of dugout canoes for their final push to the sea. Mackenzie and his men didn't linger at their destination because of increasing hostility from the Bella Bella people. At one point, the explorers took refuge on top of a large rock that they used as an improvised fort, forcing the Bella Bellas at musket point to keep their distance. Mackenzie just had time to mix up some ochre and bear grease to create a primitive paint and make his own mark on the landscape. He daubed on a rock "Alex Mackenzie, from Canada by land, 22d July 1793."

After travelling back across the Rockies, Mackenzie never returned to western Canada, but he did remain active in the fur trade. He fell out with Simon McTavish, who controlled the North West Company, and helped set up a rival fur-trading outfit, the New North West Company, which was known as the XY Company (see Chapter 3). The two companies competed until McTavish's death in 1804 and then merged. Mackenzie's book about his journey to the Pacific made him an instant celebrity. He was knighted and later acquired a country estate near Inverness by marrying a cousin. He died in 1820.

Mackenzie's 1200-mile expedition to and from the Pacific had taken 76 days. There was no doubt that it was an epic journey, but it was a failure because it did not produce a feasible trading route. The Nor'Westers hired another Scot to do the job properly.

Unlike Mackenzie, explorer Simon Fraser was a dour but determined man with a limited education. What they both shared was guts. Fraser had been born in Vermont in 1776, three years after his family arrived in North America from Scotland. His father, as many newly arrived Highlanders did, fought against the rebels during the American Revolution and died a prisoner of war. The remaining family moved to St. Andrews in Stormont County (next door to the Glengarry County home of the Macdonnells).

Fraser managed to get a little schooling in Montréal before joining the North West Company as a clerk in 1792. He owed the job to his mother's being a member of the Grant clan, which was already heavily involved in the fur trade, and to his late father's family ties to Simon McTavish. But Fraser proved to be more than an impoverished relation living on family handouts and showed so much talent as a trader that he was made a full partner in the company in 1802.

He was also chosen to be the Nor'Westers' man in the Athabasca country following Mackenzie's defection.

Fraser took his time building up the Nor'Westers' business on the northeastern slopes of the Rockies and established the first Canadian trading post west of the mountains at Trout Lake in 1805. He seemed to be in no hurry to find out if the Native people had been telling Mackenzie the truth when they said the Grand River could not be travelled by canoe. Fraser built a series of trading posts, including Fort George (now Prince George), in what is now northeastern British Columbia, which he named New Caledonia in honour of his parents' homeland.

Fraser loathed Mackenzie. Fraser's journals from the time are full of swipes at the other explorer, whom he accused of incompetence. He questioned how Mackenzie could have missed Trout Lake and noted: "It does not appear to have been noticed by Sir A M K as he used to indulge himself in a little sleep." Meow.

Eventually, in 1808, he set off down Mackenzie's mysterious river with four canoes, accompanied by his Scottish sidekick John Stuart, Canadien trader Jules Quesnel, 19 voyageurs and two Native guides. It didn't take long to verify what the Natives had told Mackenzie. Fraser and his men found themselves riding on one of the most turbulent rivers in North America. The river had too many rapids to make it navigable for trade. When Fraser reached Hell's Gate, he was forced to abandon his canoes. The explorers had to use the web of ropes and tree trunks the Natives used to move along the steep canyon wall. On the other side of the canyon, Fraser hired some dugout canoes and continued downriver to a point where it became tidal and there was a tang of salt in the air.

Hostile men of the Musqueam nation barred the group's access to the final few miles to the sea and persuaded Fraser to turn back.

His bosses in Montréal believed the Grand River was actually the Columbia River, but Fraser realized he was too far north for the river to be the Columbia. He too had failed in his mission to find either the headwaters of the Columbia or a practical route from the BC Interior. What he did find was the river that would mark the barrier to American expansion up the Pacific Coast. Mackenzie's Grand River came to be known as the Fraser River, and the Rockies remained a major obstacle to east-west trade until the coming of the Canadian Pacific Railway (CPR), nearly 80 years after Fraser and his men canoed to the coast.

In the meantime, the search for a route to the Orient came to focus on the Arctic and the fabled Northwest Passage. European explorers had been sailing west in the hope of reaching the Far East since the late 1400s. Christopher Columbus thought he'd reached the East Indies when he arrived in the Caribbean. That's why he called the local people "Indians." When Henry Hudson sailed into Hudson Bay, he thought he'd found the fabled Northwest Passage, but instead of a seaway to the riches of the east, he'd actually discovered a massive dead end.

The search for the Northwest Passage was revived around 1817 when some Scottish whaling ship captains operating around the Davis Strait and into the eastern fringes of the Arctic reported an unprecedented breakup in the pack ice. The British were eager to find the long-predicted seaway across the top of Canada from the Atlantic to the Pacific. The Royal Navy chose Galloway sailor John Ross to probe the maze of ice-bound islands, bays and headlands that made up the eastern Arctic for a clear passage to the Mackenzie River and the Bering Strait beyond.

Ross was an experienced, battle-scarred Royal Navy veteran who carried no fewer than 13 wounds from sea fights with the French and their allies. In 1818, he sailed the whaler *Isabella*, pressed into Royal Navy service, up the Davis Strait and then turned west to begin the search for a route to the Pacific. He failed dismally. He wrongly declared that Smith Sound, to the north of Baffin Bay, and Jones Sound to the east were both bays and failed to explore them properly. His biggest mistake was to conclude that Lancaster Sound was also a bay. He went so far as to name the mountain range at its far end in honour of John Croker, a British naval official. Ross then sailed back to Britain. The mountains were a mirage that failed to fool many of his officers, who disagreed with Ross's decision to turn back.

The following year, Ross's deputy, William Parry, sailed through Lancaster Sound and got as far as Melville Island before being halted by the pack ice. Among Parry's crew was Ross's nephew James Ross. He had been on his uncle's original expedition and was now rewarded for his contribution to Parry's voyage by having one of the headlands on Melville Island named in his honour.

By 1836, James Ross had spent eight winters in the Arctic on expeditions seeking the Northwest Passage. His fourth trip, in 1824, was a disaster. The ship he was on, the *Fury*, was forced aground on Somerset Island and had to be abandoned. Ross was also part of an 1827 attempt to drag boats across the Arctic ice from where it began, 100 miles north of Spitsbergen

Island, to a non-existent sea believed to be near the North Pole. Once again, the expedition was a disaster. For every 10 miles the men dragged the boats, the ice drifted six miles south. After taking five days to move one mile north, the expedition was abandoned 500 miles from the North Pole. No one got any closer to the pole until 1875, when members of the British Arctic Expedition under Captain George S. Nares went farther north.

Meanwhile, back in Britain, John Ross was driven by the constant criticism of his first expedition to try again. He convinced fellow Galloway man Felix Booth, who had made a fortune selling gin, to finance the first steamship expedition into Arctic waters. James Ross was persuaded to come on the expedition, and uncle and nephew teamed up for what turned out to be a marathon four years trapped on ice floes. The steamship *Victory* was caught in the ice in Prince Regent Inlet, and the crew survived by scavenging supplies from James Ross's old ship, the *Fury*, on nearby Somerset Island. James Ross showed a willingness to listen to and learn from local people—a trait often possessed by Scottish explorers in contrast to their English counterparts—and managed to keep his men free of the dreaded vitamin-deficiency disease scurvy by feeding them a high-fat Inuit diet. He also managed a 28-day sledge trip that located the Magnetic North Pole in 1831.

After four and a half years, the Rosses and their men were rescued by a whaling ship that turned out to be the old *Isabella*, which John Ross had captained during his first Arctic expedition. Only three members of the expedition had died, which was reckoned very good going for a British venture in those days.

James Ross was offered a knighthood for his contributions to exploration and science, but he turned it down. Then, in 1848, he received an offer he could not bring himself to refuse. Three years earlier, Royal Navy explorer Sir John Franklin had gone missing along with 129 men after entering Arctic waters. His distraught widow, Lady Franklin, asked Ross to lead a search expedition. Ross failed to find Franklin, but the explorer did map another 150 miles of northern Canada's coastline.

Franklin's widow may have loved her husband, but experienced Arctic hands found little to admire in him apart from his quiet courage. Dr. John Richardson, a Royal Navy doctor from Dumfries, was on Franklin's 1819 expedition to reach the Arctic via the Coppermine River. Franklin and Richardson reached the mouth of the Coppermine but almost starved to death on the shores of Great Bear Lake. Richardson had to take charge and executed one of the voyageurs on the expedition for killing a British sailor. The voyageur was a suspected cannibal. By the time local Natives rescued the Franklin party, nine of its members were dead from starvation or exposure. Meanwhile, Franklin refused to walk more than 8 miles a day, and his aggressive and snobbish attitude alienated fur traders and Natives alike. On his return to England in 1822, however, Franklin was treated as a hero. He was, after all, a gentleman. Breeding rather than brains was the most important quality in a true leader, at least as far as the Royal Navy was concerned.

Despite Franklin's blundering, Richardson agreed to be the stuffy explorer's second-in-command when he returned to the Arctic in 1824. By 1826, Richardson had mapped 900 miles of Arctic coastline from the Mackenzie River to the Coppermine River. His maps were later crucial to the successful navigation of the Northwest Passage.

Richardson was lucky that he was too busy improving care for the mentally ill in Britain, pioneering the use of anaesthesia in surgery and becoming one of the most highly regarded biologists of his time to go on Franklin's final, fatal, expedition. He did, however, join forces with the greatest of all the Scottish Arctic explorers, John Rae, in 1848 to search for Franklin. That journey failed to find any trace of the Royal Navy explorers, but it was the beginning of a series of events that would make Rae one of the most hated men in England.

Unlike most of the other Arctic explorers, Rae did not come from a mentally stultified Royal Navy background. He was the son of the Hudson's Bay Company agent in Orkney. The fur company's ships stopped off in the harbour at Stromness in the early 1800s to pick up last-minute perishable supplies and, more importantly, Orcadians to work at HBC trading posts in Canada. Rae was born in 1813 and was a qualified doctor by 1833, when he followed his father and two older brothers into the employ of the fur company.

His skills as a doctor and survival expert were challenged when the ship carrying him out of Hudson Bay was turned back by ice in the Hudson Strait, and its passengers were forced to winter at Charlton Island in James Bay. The dreaded scurvy broke out, and two crewmen died before Rae discovered a source of vital vitamin C in cranberries preserved under the snow.

Rae had joined the HBC in search of adventure, and he was soon pestering the Cree people around the trading post at Moose Factory for travelling and hunting tips. Former colleague Robert Ballantyne was amazed at Rae's skill on snowshoes and reckoned him "the best and ablest snowshoe walker not only in the Hudson Bay Territory but also of the age."

"He [is] very muscular and active," noted Ballantyne, "full of animal spirits, and has a fine intellectual countenance—he does not proceed as other expeditions have done, with many large supplies of provisions and ten or twelve men....The party are to depend almost entirely on their guns and provisions...and penetrate into these unexplored regions on foot."

As well as respecting the survival skills of the Cree, Rae was also deeply interested in their culture and became a keen collector of Native artifacts, which he sent home to museums in Scotland.

In 1844, HBC's top man in Canada at the time, fellow Scot Sir George Simpson, picked Rae to explore the northern barrens. But Rae decided he needed to learn more about surveying and navigation first. He canoed from Moose Factory to Fort Garry (present-day Winnipeg) to study, but shortly after he arrived, his teacher died. So the Scot walked 1200 miles east to Sault Ste. Marie and boarded a boat that took him via the Great Lakes to Toronto, where he found another teacher.

Rae finally reached the Arctic in 1846 and soon logged the first of many distinctions in his career when he and the members of his expedition became the first white men to spend the winter on land in the High Arctic. The party of 11 HBC men at the base of the Melville Peninsula adopted the diet and hunting methods taught by their two Inuit guides to make it through the winter. Burning bog plants for fuel was also an innovation for white explorers. The expedition determined that Boothia was not an island and that the sea passage must lie farther north.

After the failure of his joint expedition with Richardson to find Franklin, Rae tried to settle back into his work as a fur trader but found himself restless. "It is certain that I was never intended for a man of business, and my avocations for the last four or five years have driven what little I did know about accounts, etc., quite out of my head," he wrote to a colleague.

Rae's thirst for action was quenched in 1850 when Simpson ordered him to go on a second expedition to find Franklin. Rae had two boats built that were specially designed for navigating the waters of the High Arctic, but thick ice prevented their reaching King William Island. All Rae had to show for his efforts were two pieces of wood that he believed, probably correctly, came from one of Franklin's two ships.

Rae was back in the Arctic in 1853, and he and his six fellow searchers learned from the Inuit how to build snow houses and survive a winter on Repulse Bay. In March 1854, Rae and his men headed west and soon began to learn the truth about the last days of the Franklin expedition. Inuit they met told them of a large group of white men who starved to death farther along the coast. Rae was even able to trade for items, such as monogrammed silverware and a kettle, that obviously belonged to Franklin and his men. The Inuit also told Rae something no one in England wanted to hear. The last survivors from Franklin's expedition had resorted to cannibalism before they died.

When Rae repeated in England what he had been told, he was met by a fierce storm of anger and disbelief. Officially, Englishmen did not eat Englishmen. In fact, it was an old custom of the sea that cannibalism was acceptable as a last resort so long as lots were drawn to decide who would be dinner and the weakest member of the party wasn't simply murdered for the pot.

Rae was heavily criticized for failing to visit the scene of the final tragedy, even though it was too late in the season to go there, and he was subjected to a smear campaign organized by Lady Franklin that involved the famous novelist Charles Dickens. There was a £10,000 reward for anyone with information about the fate of Franklin and his expedition, but the explorer's widow fought hard to prevent Rae's receiving it. Two years later, Rae was grudgingly awarded £8000, and the balance of the reward money was split between the other members of his search team. Rae never returned to the Arctic, and much of the map work he did there was credited to a Royal Navy officer.

What Rae had said about cannibalism was proved true when the remains of Franklin's men were finally found. There were deep cuts made by steel knives in many of the men's bones, and one bone had been completely sawed through. As well, recent studies of tissue taken from the frozen bodies of the men who died early in the expedition reveal high levels of lead. It is believed that the lead solder used to seal the expedition's tinned food partially poisoned them. The navy men would have been far better to follow Rae's example and live off the land like the Inuit. No wonder Rae branded the Royal Navy's officers "donkeys."

While Rae received little recognition in his own lifetime, especially after he revealed the terrible truth about the Franklin expedition, he was widely admired by the generation of explorers who followed and finally conquered the Arctic. Roald Amundsen and Vilhjalmur Stefansson were fans of Rae, and when Amundsen finally sailed through the Northwest Passage in 1903, he named the long-sought strait that made the voyage possible in Rae's honour.

But it wasn't only the Royal Navy and the Hudson's Bay Company who were active in the Arctic in the days of Ross and Rae. Whaling crews, many of them made up of Scots sailing out of Aberdeen, Peterhead and Dundee, were probing deep into the ice floes, looking for an Arctic base, close to the whales, that would give them a commercial edge over their American competitors. In 1840, Aberdeen skipper William Penny took the first ship into Cumberland Sound since John Davis visited the area in 1587. Penny commanded one of the 30 expeditions sent to look for Franklin.

Another Scot who joined the search for Franklin was ex-HBC man William Kennedy, who had quit the company because it was selling booze to the Natives. Lady Franklin hired him to lead a search expedition in 1851. Kennedy didn't find Franklin, but he did reach Prince Regent Bay, where he used gunpowder to blast his way through the ice.

One of the least likely Scots to explore the Canadian north was Robert Campbell from Glen Lyon in Perthshire. He was hired by the HBC in 1830 to look after a flock of sheep the company was importing from Kentucky to pasture on the banks of the Red River. The experiment was a failure, so Campbell decided to try his hand at fur trading. The HBC sent him to explore the country west of the Mackenzie River, and Campbell is credited with discovering the Yukon River in 1842. Of course, the Chilkat people knew all about the river, and they resented the fact that Campbell built a fort at its junction with the Pelly River. They showed their displeasure by destroying Campbell's Fort Selkirk in 1852.

Campbell was perhaps too cautious a man to make the same kind of mark as many of the other Scottish explorers, but he did share with them the bloody-minded determination and willingness to take advice that drove them to the very fringes of what would become Canada and helped define the shape of a nation.

HAGGIS

Some would say it's fortunate that the Scots haven't had much of an effect on Canadian cuisine. Instead, the Scots who came to Canada decided to embrace alternatives to a diet based on oatmeal, potatoes, salted herring, milk, animal blood and the bits of animals no one else wanted to eat. Strangely, the wheel has gone full circle and those self-same bits of animal are now popular in Canada in the guise of burgers. But that old Scots favourite, black, or blood, pudding, is hidden away with the other "ethnic" foods on supermarket shelves. That's if you can get it at all.

Maybe more people should go back to the Scottish diet—the old Scottish diet, that is, with perhaps more fresh fruit and vegetables. Modern Scots are said to have one of the worst diets in the world, an unhealthy mixture of fried and highly processed foods. For goodness' sake, they even deep-fry chocolate bars!

Apart from the deep-fried chocolate bar, Scotland's most famous (or infamous) contribution to world cuisine is haggis. The haggis is not, as commonly claimed, a Highland creature with two legs shorter than the other two, which allow it to run quickly along mountain crags. It's basically the bits of an animal you wouldn't eat if you could recognize them. Traditionally, haggis is served with boiled and mashed turnip.

To make haggis you have to befriend a butcher. One of the main ingredients in haggis is suet, which most Canadian supermarkets only seem to stock around Christmastime.

Haggis is supposed to be made in a sheep's stomach, though it may be easier to buy a large-diameter sausage skin at a specialty store. If you can find a sheep stomach, wash it well in cold water and scrape it clean with a sharp knife. Then soak the stomach overnight in cold, slightly salted water.

If you take the real-sheep-stomach route, you also need to get the pluck (i.e., the lungs, heart and liver) with the windpipe still attached. Boil the pluck for two hours with the windpipe hanging over the side of the pot. Put a can under the windpipe to catch any drips. After two hours, pull the pluck out of the pot and put it in a basin. Then pour the cooking water over it and leave to soak overnight. Throw the stuff in the drip-can out.

Okay, in the morning you've got to cut the windpipe off the pluck, grate the liver and mince the heart and lungs. Keep the water the pluck was soaked in. Chop up about a quarter pound of suet and mix it in with the grated liver and minced heart and lungs. Now take four onions, peel them and put the whole onions into cold water. Heat the water until it boils, then take the onions out and plunge them into cold water. Finally, chop the onions into fine bits and add them to the mix.

You also have to toast about half a pound of oatmeal. That's rolled oatmeal, not the quick or instant variety. Add the oatmeal to the mix along with a couple of tablespoons of salt. Throw in some pepper and a few of your favourite herbs. Now take about a pint of the water the pluck was boiled in and add it to the mix. Massage the whole lot till it forms a goo and put it into the sheep stomach or sausage skin. (If you've gone with sausage skin, you've probably also opted to buy the heart, liver and lungs on their own and not bothered with the pluck.) Half fill the bag and then sew it closed. Prick the bag a couple of times to let the air out, as the mixture will expand. Put the bag in boiling water and leave it for three hours to simmer. It's advisable to keep an eye on the bag and prick it again if it looks like it's going to explode.

For those who don't have 24 hours to make a meal, there's Quick Haggis. For this, you just need to finely chop four ounces of suet and warm it in a saucepan until it melts. Add a chopped onion and let it fry in the suet. Then add eight ounces of lightly toasted oatmeal along with some salt and pepper. Put the lid on the saucepan and let the mixture cook slowly for about 20 minutes.

Haggis used to be served as part of the school dinner program in Scotland. Fish-and-chip shops still serve haggis—deep fried, of course.

A Scots recipe that is far less hassle and is just as traditional is Potato Scones. This is really easy. First, boil up a potato or two. Mash the potato with a little butter. Then start adding flour, mixed with a pinch of baking powder, to the mashed potato until you get a ball with the consistency of dry dough. Make several balls from the "dough" and flatten them. Make sure the scones are reasonably thin, and prick them with a fork. Then put them in a frying pan with just a smear of oil and cook them on both sides. When the scones are mottled brown, take them out of the pan and enjoy them. These go really well with a fried egg and some fried slices of blood pudding.

CHAPTER SIX

NEW WORLD,
NEW HOPE

There are no trees in Canada that produce tea, soap and sugar. But the existence of such a miraculous tree was one of many lies invented by the ruthless men running the emigration business to part Scots from their money in the late 1700s and early 1800s.

The Scots who came to Canada did find a sugar-producing tree, the maple, which may have been miraculous enough for them. And a sweet miracle would no doubt have been welcome after a six-week voyage on ships that were frequently squalid hulks on which diseases such as cholera and typhoid took their grim harvests from the weakest, the old and the young. When the Scots settlers arrived, they often found not the beautifully laid-out townships lying among verdant fields that were promised, but tents surrounded by gloomy forest as far as the eye could penetrate.

Even settlers with farming experience found life hard. The crops they grew in Scotland were far different from the ones they were expected to produce in Canada, and the first thing many had to do was learn to swing an axe and begin clearing the land. Felling forests was something few people in Scotland had been asked to do for hundreds of years.

The Highlanders who swarmed through the surf at Pictou in 1773, many wearing the kilts outlawed in their homeland, were shocked to be confronted with a solid wall of trees broken only by a few pitiful settler shacks. The voyage from Loch Broom in northwest Scotland had already been a nightmare for the 189 passengers on the *Hector*. The old Dutch brig's timbers were so rotten they could be picked away with a fingernail, and the ship seemed to take forever to cross the Atlantic. After ten weeks, almost a month longer than the average crossing, the ship was caught in a storm off Newfoundland and blown back out to sea. It took another two weeks to get to Pictou. By that time, 18 of the 70 children on board were dead from disease, and everyone was living on mouldy crumbs one of the more prudent passengers had saved from happier times.

The *Hector*'s arrival in mid-September meant that the settlers had no time to prepare themselves for the winter. The Philadelphia Company, which owned Pictou, was unsympathetic to their requests for help, so the Highlanders marched to the settlement agent's shack and carried him to the company storehouse, where they took what they needed and gave him IOU notes. Even with the supplies, life was tough for the *Hector*'s settlers, and many of the men and older children made their way to Halifax and Irish-dominated

Truro to sell themselves as virtual slaves in a bid to get the money to see their families through the winter. Things got easier after that first winter, and the settlers and the Highlanders who followed them were to put a distinctly Scottish stamp on Nova Scotia. The *Hector* took on the same status as the *Mayflower* did for many Americans.

Of course, the *Hector* settlers were not the first Scots in Canada by a long stretch. There had been Scots in the country from nearly the first days of white settlement. Nova Scotia, which got its name from a failed Scottish attempt to create a New Scotland on the northern Atlantic seaboard in the 1620s, became French territory, Acadia, in 1632 (see Chapter 2). A handful of Scots remained on the island under French rule and married into Acadian families, but their descendants were scattered to the four winds in 1755 when Britain, which had regained control of the island in 1713, expelled the Acadians. When the British returned, so did the name Nova Scotia. The majority of settlers who took over the Acadian farms were New Englanders, though many of them had Scottish roots. Their ancestors had settled in the north of Ireland during the rule of James I before uprooting themselves again to move to New Hampshire.

The Philadelphia Company sent six families, two of them Scottish, to Pictou in 1767. Renfrew settler Robert Patterson brought an eight-day clock in addition to his wife and five children, while John Rogers from Glasgow brought a bag of appleseeds, a wife and five children. A condition of settlement was that they cultivate hemp, which was to be made into rope for the Royal Navy.

Highland soldiers who had fought against the French were given land along the St. Lawrence River to establish a British presence in the territory signed over in the 1763 Treaty of Paris. Plans were also well in hand to colonize Prince Edward Island. In 1786, the island was divided up into 67 townships that were parcelled out to a number of landlords, many of them Scottish ex-army officers, for development. However, the new owners preferred land speculation to actual settlement, and by 1779, only 16 of the townships were being farmed. Many of the farmers were Scots.

Highland chieftain Captain John MacDonald sold his land at Glenaladale in Scotland and used the money to buy two townships in the Tracadie area, where he settled 300 people from the Moydart and Uist areas in 1772. He paid the settlers' passage and gave them free clothing, tools and a year's worth of supplies. He didn't receive much gratitude, especially when some of the supplies he'd ordered failed to show up. Life was hard on the island for the settlers, and not all the landowners shared MacDonald's concern for their welfare. Lord Advocate Sir James Montgomery, the most senior law officer in Scotland, sneered at the 120 families of Perthshire Scots who took up his offer of land at one shilling per acre, calling them "white Negroes."

The port of Campbeltown, at the southern end of Argyll, was another popular source of immigrants to PEI. Most were luckier than the passengers on the *Elizabeth*, which broke loose from its moorings in 1775 and was driven ashore in a storm. All passengers survived the shipwreck, but their supplies and belongings were lost. More than 70 years later, the safety of the sea voyage hadn't much improved.

Between 1847 and 1853, no fewer than 49 ships sank while on their way to Canada.

In 1774, Lockerbie man Wellwood Waugh brought a parcel of settlers to PEI from the Dumfries and Selkirk areas of the Scottish borders. Four years later, they moved to Pictou after locusts destroyed their crop on PEI. Observers in Pictou noted the Borderers seemed smarter and harder working than the Highlanders who already lived there. That may seem a harsh judgement when we recall that few of the Highlanders could speak or read English. On the other hand, the Highlanders came from what had been, until only shortly before, a warrior society, where the drudge work was left to the women. To counter this, some observers suggested it might help to mix Highlanders and Lowlanders together. They noted that Highlanders were so used to poverty that they were easily satisfied and tended to do the bare minimum of work needed to survive. But when the Highlanders had Lowlanders for neighbours, their competitive instincts kicked in and they strove to outshine them in developing their farms.

Prince Edward Island received a fresh influx of Highland blood in 1803 when Scottish nobleman and social reformer Lord Selkirk sent out 800 settlers, mainly from Skye and Ross-shire, with a sprinkling from Uist and Argyll. Selkirk believed the solution to overcrowding and poverty in the Highlands was not to sentence Highlanders to industrial servitude in the growing slums of Glasgow, but to establish them on farms in Canada where they could enjoy something resembling their traditional lifestyle. He sold them his land on the island for a low price, or even on credit, and brought in more Highlanders in 1804 and 1808.

Despite plagues of mice and grasshoppers that destroyed the crops, the rich red soil of PEI proved fruitful for the Highlanders, and Selkirk's settlements were a great success. He was less successful at Baldoon in Ontario and Red River in Manitoba.

Meanwhile, Pictou had received a further population boost after the American Revolution, when more than 120 Scottish soldiers from Hamilton's Regiment settled in the area. Life was still harsh there. Shortly after the ex-soldiers arrived, the Reverend James MacGregor described the area as basically forest with a scattering of "mean timber" shacks to be seen here and there. It was this unappetizing prospect that persuaded 400 settlers, who arrived from Loch Broom in 1817 under the leadership of the Reverend Norman MacLeod, not to linger. About half of them followed MacLeod to St. Ann's Harbour in Cape Breton and then across the Pacific to Australia and finally New Zealand.

Scottish immigration to Canada increased rapidly after the end of the war against France that began in 1793 and raged almost constantly until 1815. During the war, Highlanders had been employed picking seaweed, which was used to produce essential chemicals, and fighting the French. The area's young men had shouldered much of the burden of supplying soldiers to the army. In the wake of the war, Britain, and the Highlands in particular, was plunged into an economic depression. Cheaper supplies of the chemicals were available from overseas, and the landlords decided to turn their hills and glens into sheep farms. The unemployed seaweed workers and soldiers flooded into the industrial areas of Lowland Scotland and undercut their southern cousins on the labour market. The stage was set for a massive wave of emigration from Scotland.

Between 1815 and 1838, Scots accounted for 22,000 of the 39,000 immigrants who landed in Nova Scotia. Many of the Highlanders headed to Cape Breton, where there were solid pockets of fellow Gaelic speakers. Unfortunately, the soil in many parts of Cape Breton was as bad as the soil back in Scotland. When it failed to produce a good living, the children of the Highland immigrants drifted into the booming coal and steel industries. Around the same time, their Scottish cousins were doing much the same thing in the mines and foundries of industrial Scotland. But the Cape Breton Highlanders, unlike the Scots who remained at home, retained more of their ancestors' culture. The sound of Gaelic was heard in Cape Breton long after it stopped echoing along the mean streets of industrialized Scotland.

The Highlanders who went to Ontario were quicker to lose their native tongue and adopt English than the Cape Bretoners. They arrived after the War of 1812 made the British government realize that Upper Canada needed to be populated with settlers sympathetic to Britain if it was to stay out of American hands. The authorities decided that they wanted more people like the Glengarry Highlanders in Upper Canada. Scotland had plenty of people to spare now that the wars against the French were at an end, and the British government's attitude to emigration had changed. Previously it had actively discouraged emigration, particularly of men with skills, but now it was seen as an excellent way to dump excess population on Canada.

By 1819, almost one-third of the families in Lanarkshire, the industrial heartland of Scotland, were on some kind of welfare, and in the 1820s the British government began making easy-term loans of £100 per household to Scottish families willing to emigrate. The primitive trade unions got into the act, in a bid to reduce competition for jobs and push up wages, and set up societies that encouraged emigration. Canada was inundated with unemployed Scottish black-smiths, carpenters and weavers trying to be farmers.

Many Scots proved to be more cautious than their English and Irish cousins when it came to going into farming. Instead of clearing their own land, the Scots settlers preferred to get a job and earn the money to buy a "made farm" or pay Canadians or Americans, who were already handy with axes, to take down the trees for them. The idea of farming as a full-time job is a surprisingly recent phenomenon; in the 1800s, everyone who could afford to buy land, from doctors to clerks, had a farm.

Responsibility for encouraging settlement on Crown land was put in the hands of private companies that received substantial grants in exchange for establish-ing communities. There were also big profits to be made in supplying the new settlers with provisions. The colonization companies sent their agents to scour Scotland for possible settlers. Once recruited, the new emigrants were funnelled to the west coast ports of Glasgow and Greenock for shipment to Montréal. Then the settlers made their way by barge, sled or cart to their new homes in the heavily wooded wilderness.

Some colonization companies did a better job than others. Irishman Thomas Talbot realized that many of the settlements were failing because Ontario lacked a proper road network. Early Scots settlers lamented that their farm yields were half what they'd been told they'd get, but the cost of bringing in supplies was twice what they'd budgeted because of the poor transportation system. Talbot insisted, as a condition of settlement, that each farmer had to build a road alongside half the length of his property. The farmer's neighbour built the other half.

Many of Talbot's settlers in southwestern Ontario came from Argyll and Perthshire. He believed them to be lazy, drunken and shiftless, so he may not have been over the moon when 140 Highland refugees from Lord Selkirk's Red River colony arrived on his doorstep. They had been driven off their land by Métis, working for the fur traders of the North West Company, who were opposed to any attempt to farm on what they regarded as their territory. Unfortunately for Talbot, he had been settling some of the Highlanders on Crown land to which he had no legal right. The resulting five-year legal squabble further soured Talbot's opinion of Highlanders, but at least he didn't end up in jail. Donald Cameron spent a lot of his own money bringing 600 Scots settlers to the Eddon and Thorah areas, but he was jailed for fraud because he didn't bring as many settlers as he'd told the authorities he had.

The colonization agents preferred to recruit neighbours in Scotland to become neighbours in Canada. This arrangement suited the Scots as well. William Dickson had little problem finding settlers from the Scottish borders for his Dundee Township at the western end of Lake Ontario in 1816. Within 20 years, it boasted 6000 souls. The same year Dundee was founded, the highly successful settlement of Perth was also established. Communities with Scottish names were springing up throughout what would become Ontario. Along the north shore of Lake Erie were townships with such names as Wallacetown, Campbelltown, Fingal, Crinan and Glencoe.

One of the biggest colonization outfits was the Canada Company, which in 1826 had appointed Scottish novelist John Galt to settle a 1.1-million-acre area known as the Huron Tract. Galt and his sidekick William "Tiger" Dunlop proved so capable at attracting Scots that they persuaded many who had intended to head for the United States to settle in Goderich and Seaforth. Although John Galt succeeded in attracting 2000 settlers to Guelph, only half of the Huron Tract was populated by 1837, and his bosses were getting impatient. Dunlop had deserted him and was actually campaigning against the company, and Galt found himself in trouble for putting people before profit. The company had been far from impressed by the easy terms he gave a group of Scottish settlers who turned up in Guelph after a disastrous attempt to create a farm colony in Venezuela. Galt was eventually fired. (Galt's son Alexander, a Father of Confederation, and his grandson Elliott were settlement promoters a generation later and played a large part in populating the area around Lethbridge, Alberta.)

There were basically two types of Scottish immigrant coming to Canada around this time: the voluntary immigrants, usually Lowlanders with readily marketable skills; and the Highlanders, who were sometimes driven onto the emigrant ships by thugs in the pay of brutal and callous landowners. The Lowlanders had the advantage of speaking English, and they tended to find good jobs. The 1861 census in Montréal found the majority of Scots had white-collar jobs or worked as skilled tradesmen. Only 14 percent were unskilled labourers, and 17 percent were in high-income jobs such as doctoring or store owning. It was the Highlanders who were the headache.

In the 1840s, a potato famine hit the Highlands and the Islands. It was nowhere near as devastating as the potato famine in Ireland, but those who could afford to get out did so. Many who couldn't afford to leave were driven out by their landlords, who faced plunging incomes when their tenants could not pay their rents. Some landlords ended up paying their tenants' way to Canada because it seemed better to get rid of them than to have them collecting welfare in Scotland. In those days, the money for poor relief, as it was called, tended to come from the pockets of the property owners of a district.

One of the most notorious of the "evict 'em and send 'em to Canada" school of landlords was Colonel John Gordon of Cluny, who bought the hereditary lands of the MacNeil clan in Barra, South Uist and Benbecula in the late 1840s. In 1851, more than 1500 of his tenants were dumped in Montréal. The Scots of the city were appalled at the plight of their countrymen and rallied to raise money to help them. The *Quebec Times*, meanwhile, condemned Gordon. "The fifteen hundred souls whom Colonel Gordon has sent to Québec this season have all been supported for the past week at least and conveyed to Upper Canada at the expense of the colony; and at their arrival at Toronto and Hamilton, the greater number have been dependent on the charity of the benevolent for a morsel of bread," it noted. What the paper didn't know was that 400 more of Gordon's tenants were already on their way to the city.

In 1849, the *Scotsman* newspaper estimated that 20,000 Highlanders had gone to Canada in the previous decade. Of course, not all had been brutally driven onto the waiting emigrant ships. There were just as many Gaelic songs celebrating the opportunities Canada offered for escape from landlord oppression as there were laments for homes burning onshore as the ship's sails billowed with the wind that would drive the exiles across the Atlantic.

The Eastern Townships of Québec proved a magnet for people from the Isle of Lewis in the early 1840s. In 1841, the town of Sherbrooke faced the influx of 229 destitute people from Lewis. The Canadian authorities were keen to create a buffer between the Americans and the Canadiens on the St. Lawrence, so the government collected money from the merchants of Montréal and settled the Lewis Islanders in the nearby townships of Winslow and Lingwick.

In 1844, Lewis was bought by Sir James Matheson (who had made his money as a result of the Opium War, which forced the Chinese government to accept imports of opium from India). Matheson decided many of the islanders would be better off in Canada—whether they realized it or not. Thanks to the islanders Matheson forced out, Gaelic was commonly heard in the Québec townships, and new French-speaking arrivals learned it and not English as a second language. The Lewis influence remained strong until the First World War, when many of the communities' men flocked to join the Black Watch of Canada and were killed on the battlefields of Europe. Without the young men to work the farms, the old Lewis families sold out to their French neighbours. When the Ford Motor Company launched a recruiting drive in the townships in the 1920s, it drew away many of the war survivors, and the Scots' strong belief in the benefits of education led to the near extinction of Gaelic in the area. A number of the descendants of the Lewis settlers who remain in the Eastern Townships now speak only French.

As the dark, brooding forests of Ontario were transformed into lush green pastures, many of the Scots looked west for new worlds to conquer. The grandchildren of the settlers who had flooded into Ontario after 1815 began to move out onto the Prairies to break fresh farmland. Some Scottish Ontarians went even farther than the Prairies and crossed the Rockies into British Columbia. A group of 150 Ontarians, along with a sprinkling of Québecers, walked 1500 miles overland from Winnipeg to the Cariboo gold fields in 1862. When the gold rush ended, the Overlanders, as the mainly Scots group was known, settled down to provide the infant British colony with many of its leading citizens. They began networking and organizing and by 1865 had formed the Vancouver St. Andrew's Society. Cowichan Bay on Vancouver Island also proved a magnet for the Scots and includes among its pioneer settlers men with such names as Bell, Duncan, Flett, McKay and Montgomery.

But it was on the Prairies that the Ontario Scots congregated. The 1872 Dominion Lands Act offered 160 acres to anyone prepared to cultivate and live on the land for three years. It was too good an offer to pass up. Although much of the settlement was done by individual families, sometimes whole communities hit the westward trail. A number of people from Paisley, who settled in Perth in 1817, moved first to Bruce County, where they established the township of Paisley in the 1850s, then 20 years later migrated to Manitoba, where they built another Paisley. The Manitoba Paisley eventually became known as Pilot Mound.

The Prairies also attracted a fresh wave of immigrants from Scotland itself. Between 1885 and 1907 there was a steady influx of Scots settlers into the Wolsley region of Saskatchewan. Moffat was the focal point of settlement for these newcomers, who were mainly from Ayrshire, Perthshire, Aberdeenshire and the area around Edinburgh. In the year ending June 30, 1904, just over 12,600 Scots came to Canada. Almost 3400 of them went to Manitoba, while 1000 headed for the area of the North-West Territories that would, one year later, become Alberta and Saskatchewan. British Columbia attracted 450 of the Scots immigrants. About 1000 of the Scots filed for homesteads for themselves and their families, and only 171 signed on to work as farm labourers. A similar survey in 1909 revealed the West was becoming even more popular with the Scots. Of the 11,810 arrivals, about 1890 went to Manitoba, almost as many went to Alberta and Saskatchewan, and immigration to British Columbia was up threefold, to 1495. By 1911, nearly one in six people on the Prairies was a Scot. Banff and Carstairs, Alberta, were common destinations for Scots, and by 1941, one in four people in those communities identified themselves as Scottish.

In fact, the Scots had been quick off the mark when it came to settling on the Prairies. A survey for the years 1884 to 1885 showed that of the 28,000 non-Aboriginals in the North-West Territories, almost 6790 claimed to be Scots, and an additional 762 Métis had Scots heritage. The bulk of the Scots were living in the Broadview and Regina areas. The Canadian government's decision to encourage Ukrainian immigration to the Prairies changed the face of many of the communities, which slowly lost their Scottish feel.

The Ukrainians were better grain farmers because of their generations of farming experience on the steppes of their homeland, and they gradually eased the Scots out.

Attempts to settle crofter-fishermen on the Prairies failed to take hold. The daughter of the infamous Colonel John Gordon, who had dumped so many of his tenants on the Montréal dockside, took a slightly more humanitarian view 40 years later. Lady Cathcart arranged for 300 of her tenants to be transported to settlements near Moosimin and Wapella in Saskatchewan, but she still charged 6 percent interest on the £500 loans she made to the poor islanders so they could tide themselves over until they established their farms. The land proved to be poor, and it was not helped by an 1884 drought. As soon as the young men mastered English, many of them headed to the cities and British Columbia to look for work. But the Cathcart experiment convinced the British government to establish two communities on the Prairies. Many of the settlers for this endeavour came from Lewis, which was now owned by Lady Matheson, widow of the opium dealer who bought the island in 1844. When the islanders tried to discuss their grievances with Lady Matheson, she took herself off to Paris, and two Royal Navy gunboats landed soldiers on the island to enforce her rule.

The government sponsored 435 people in 79 family groups that were sent to Killarney in Manitoba and Saltcoats in Saskatchewan between 1888 and 1889. Neither settlement was a great success. Killarney storekeeper T.J. Lawlor questioned the sanity of sending the crofters at all. "Fancy a people taken away from fishing scenes and dumped upon the Prairies—

and no provision made for seed. Gaelic may be a very nice and expressive dialect but you cannot raise wheat from it, and these people had nothing else."

Not all the settlers regretted coming to Canada, though several were vocal in describing the new settlements as disasters. Angus Graham was one settler who did not feel betrayed or cheated. He toughed things out at Killarney until 1905 and wrote of Manitoba: "I think it is unequalled for beauty of its landscape and the richness of its soil; also its inhabitants, for such friendly and kind hearted people we have never met." Many of those people would have been Scots, as the Turtle Mountain area near Killarney had been settled under the auspices of the Scottish Canadian Land and Settlement Association since 1884.

Despite all the hardships and uncertainties associated with coming to Canada, the country attracted increasing numbers of Scots until after the Second World War. They found the country more sympathetic than Australia, New Zealand and the United States.

The vast majority of the four million or so Canadians who claim Scottish heritage are not descended from the hardy Highlanders who fought with Wolfe on the Plains of Abraham, or those who were dumped on a Montréal dockside by a callous Anglicized landlord in the 1840s. Scottish immigration to Canada was measured in thousands until the mid-1800s, then tens of thousands. Between 1871 and 1901, an estimated 80,000 Scots came to Canada. But it was in the first three decades of the twentieth century that the Scots arrived in the greatest numbers. Between 1901 and 1914, when the First World War began, about 240,000 Scots came to Canada from a home population of only five million. That means one in twenty Scots moved to

Canada during that 13-year period. There was another massive influx after the war, with 200,000 Scots arriving between 1919 and 1930. They found their predecessors from Auld Scotia had created a country that would both challenge and reward them.

Present-day Highlanders joke that they wish the 18th- and 19th-century landlords had been even more ruthless in clearing land to make way for sheep, and then they too would be living in a county that the United Nations frequently rates as the best in the world.

Perhaps the last word should go to a long-ago Scots immigrant who wrote that "the beef of Canada was so tough that teeth could not chew into it....But when in the old country he got beef but once a week, here he has it three times a day."

Archibald Macnab

Con men come in all shapes and sizes. Sometimes they come in the shape of a genuine clan chief.

Bewildered Highlanders, thrown off their ancestral lands by callous chiefs and dumped off ships in Montréal speaking only Gaelic and no English or French, could not believe their eyes when they were met at the docks by a piper. With the piper was a chieftain in full Highland dress who offered them a home away from home where they could live as their ancestors did.

The problem was that Archibald Macnab, 17th chief of the clan, was a cad and a con man. He had fled to Canada in the early 1820s to escape his debtors and his wife and daughter. Through his blood ties to members of the Family Compact (the alliance of English administrators and Scots merchants who ran Upper Canada), he managed to obtain an appointment as a government land agent for 80,000 acres in the Madawaska River area of the Ottawa Valley.

Macnab sent word back to his clansmen in the Glen Dochart area of Perthshire that he had found a new home for them in Canada. He even offered to pay the £35 cost of their sea passage from Scotland and provide supplies to help them get established in Canada, provided they paid him back. What he didn't explain to the first 100 settlers was that he didn't own the land and was only a colonization agent for the government. He made the newcomers sign papers that made them virtual serfs in his service and granted him the rights to the timber they cleared from what was actually their own land. They also paid him rent of a bushel of wheat per year for every acre they cleared.

Unaware of their rights, the Perthshire settlers signed the illegal documents. Macnab made frequent trips to Montréal to recruit more Highlanders fresh off the immigrant ships and was soon living the high life in his log mansion. He was appointed magistrate for the area and used his powers to arrest and evict any settler who dared challenge him. He even forbade the men to leave the settlement to find work elsewhere and vetoed any development project that did not benefit him directly. There were many complaints about him from the settlers, but his contacts with the Family Compact kept him fireproof. Macnab's house of cards began to collapse when Lord Durham arrived to investigate the causes of the 1837 rebellions. Macnab's settlers took their grievances directly to the lord, and their chieftain was soon snowed under with lawsuits. The government stepped in to take his colonization agency status away, but Macnab was litigious and actually managed to get £2000 compensation from the government for the way it had treated him. He soon squandered the money in his exile on the shores of Lake Ontario.

In 1850, he received word that his wife, whom he had abandoned almost 30 years earlier, had bought him a house in the Orkney Islands. The 70-year-old looked set to end his days crying in his whisky as his personal piper played laments, but one woman wasn't enough for the rogue, and he installed two local women in the family home as his mistresses and got a third woman pregnant. Macnab fled to France, where he died at the age of 80. Meanwhile, back in Canada, the settlement he started, now free of Macnab's grasping hands, thrived as a farming and lumber community.

RED RIVER BLUES

The Highlanders who settled at Red River in the early 1800s must rate as some of the unluckiest Scots ever to set foot in Canada.

Many had been victims of the notoriously brutal evictions carried out on the Duchess of Sutherland's estates in northern Scotland, where homes had been burned (one with a woman still inside) and the British Army had been called in to restore order. When the Earl of Selkirk offered them a new life on the banks of the Red River, the Highlanders must have believed the dream of a life far from the clutches of English landlords had come true. They could not foresee that they would be caught up in a vicious turf war between rival fur-trading concerns, the Montréal-based North West Company and the London-based Hudson's Bay Company, and driven from their homes again.

Thomas Douglas, fifth Earl of Selkirk, was a dreamer and an intellectual who included among his friends the famous Scottish romantic novelist Sir Walter Scott. Douglas was also a sickly man, but his six elder brothers were even sicklier, so he inherited the earldom in the southwest of Scotland in 1799. The earl had long been appalled by the social and economic upheaval in the Highlands that saw thousands of people evicted from their homes every year.

Selkirk's solution was to create a haven for the evicted Highlanders in Canada. In 1803, the earl took a group of 800 Highlanders, mostly from the Isle of Skye, to Prince Edward Island, where he settled them successfully. A year later, a similar scheme at Baldoon in Ontario failed as a result of bad management. The land they were to settle also turned out to be a swamp.

During his time in Canada, Selkirk met the Scots who ran the fur trade in Montréal and learned from them of the wonders of western Canada. The Scottish nobleman soon began buying shares in the Hudson's Bay Company, which held legal title to 116,000 square miles of land straddling what is now southern Manitoba, North Dakota and Minnesota. Eventually he and fellow family members had enough muscle on the HBC's board of governors to persuade them to let him have an area four times the size of Scotland for the equivalent of one modern Canadian dollar.

His Scottish friends at the North West Company in Montréal were not happy about Selkirk's scheme. They already had a trading post at the junction of the Red and Assiniboine rivers where Selkirk proposed to locate his settlement, and they firmly believed Selkirk's plan was part of a plot to ruin them hatched by the HBC. The fur traders were also opposed to farming because it would interfere with their business.

The first 20 settlers arrived in 1812 after a nightmare sea voyage and a winter spent on the shores of Hudson Bay. Their leader was Miles Macdonnell, a prickly man with little sense of diplomacy, who alienated the settlers and the Nor'Westers with equal ease. However, relations between the two groups were reasonably cordial that first winter, perhaps in part because the head of the North West Company post, Fort Gibraltar, was Macdonnell's brother-in-law. The local Salteaux tribe also made the settlers welcome.

The 1814 arrival of more than 100 settlers, mainly from the estates of the Duchess of Sutherland and her English husband, the Marquis of Stafford, was more than the Nor'Westers could stomach. But instead of harassing the settlers themselves, they persuaded some local Métis to do their dirty work for them. Most of the Métis leaders were the sons of Scots traders and Native women, and it soon became obvious that the alpha male in the pack was Cuthbert Grant. Saskatchewan-born Grant was no dummy; he had received a good education in either Scotland or Montréal before settling in the Red River area. There, his skill with a rifle and his ability to down a whole bottle of rum with no apparent ill effects earned him the admiration of the Métis.

Macdonnell threw gas on the smouldering embers of Métis resentment in 1814 when he outlawed the export of pemmican from Red River and seized pemmican supplies that were intended for the Nor'Westers. (Pemmican, a mixture of buffalo meat, berries and fat, was a staple food for fur traders in the west.) The Montréal fur traders sent Scot Duncan Cameron to convince the settlers to leave. He could speak to them in Gaelic, which Macdonnell could not, and by night he loosed Grant and his men to kill livestock, snipe at settlers and vandalize property. He even persuaded some of the settlers, dubbed "The Gardeners" by the Métis, to stage a revolt against the autocratic Macdonnell.

Another 40 Scots settlers from the Sutherland estates arrived the same year, but Cameron held an ace in his hand. The North West Company had engineered an offer of free land on Thomas Talbot's settlement in southwestern Ontario (see Chapter 6), and Cameron finally persuaded 140 of the settlers to leave the harsh winters on the prairie for what promised to be an easier life back east.

The Métis swooped down, daubed in war paint, to destroy what was left of the settlement and drive the remaining 13 families out of their homes. The settlers headed off to Norway House, the nearest HBC post, where fur trader John McLeod and three other Highlanders, Hugh Mclean, Archie Currie and James McIntosh, turned the blacksmith's shop into a small fort and held the post by firing lengths of chain from a cannon at the Métis.

By this time, Cameron had arrested Macdonnell for "stealing" the Nor'Westers' pemmican and sent him east for trial. But the next spring, a fresh wave of settlers arrived with a new governor, Robert Semple. Some of the original settlers who had left at Cameron's urging had stopped at Jack Lake, where the HBC's Colin Robertson persuaded his fellow Scots to return with him to Red River. Semple had Cameron arrested and sent east for trial, though ultimately nothing happened to him. The Nor'Westers' Fort Gibraltar was demolished, and its best timbers were taken for use at the HBC's Fort Douglas nearby.

Now the Métis, and their Nor'Wester puppet masters, moved from intimidation to murder and major arson.

The HBC post at Brandon was plundered, and canoes taking supplies to the Bay men were robbed. A few weeks later, Semple saw a group of about 60 Métis and Native people on horseback under the command of Cuthbert Grant trying to sneak past Fort Douglas for a meeting with the Nor'Westers. Gathering 25 men around him, Semple walked across the prairie to intercept the Métis at a clump of trees known as Seven Oaks. Words were exchanged, a shot was fired and there was a bloodbath as the crack-shot Métis gunned down the men on foot. Semple was shot in the leg and then blasted through the heart as he lay wounded. Few of his men managed to escape, and the bodies of the dead were mutilated. Grant later said he had counted 23 dead from Semple's party and one dead Métis.

Once again, the settlers headed north to take refuge on the shores of Lake Winnipeg. But Selkirk was already on his way with a force of Swiss mercenaries, who had come to Canada to fight for the British in the War of 1812 and were now unemployed. He stopped at Fort William, the Nor'Westers' western headquarters on the shores of Lake Superior, where he "arrested" several of the company's leading partners, including famed explorer Simon Fraser, company head William McGillivray and Dr. John McLoughlin. He also made the mistake of confiscating the furs at Fort William.

Fort Douglas was recaptured, and any of the settlers who were willing to return, yet again, from Lake Winnipeg were reinstated. Selkirk's mercenaries were invited to join the settlement, and there was an attempt to encourage Swiss immigration. The settlement survived floods and plagues of locusts, but gradually its character became more Métis than Scottish. By 1821, only 200 of the 400 people living there claimed to be Scottish.

Shortly after Semple's death, the Nor'Westers arrested Owen Keveny, an Irishman who had once been Miles Macdonnell's right-hand man at Red River and now worked for the HBC. He was murdered en route to Montréal by a former Swiss mercenary working for the Nor'Westers. The man, Charles de Reinhard, confessed and was hanged in Montréal. Strangely, out of 150 charges laid against Nor'Westers as a result of the turf war fought in the Red River country, Reinhard was the only one punished.

Selkirk found himself obstructed at every turn by the Canadian authorities, who were firmly in the pocket of the North West Company. Selkirk was fined £2000 for unlawful imprisonment and the illegal confiscation of the furs at Fort William. He left Canada a broken man in 1818 and died two years later in France at the age of 48. In 1821, the two competing fur companies merged.

More than half of the men involved in the killing of Semple and his party died violent or sudden deaths themselves. Several drowned, one impaled himself on a pitch-fork, three died from alcohol poisoning, one fell stone dead at a dance, another was killed by a bolt of lightning and three were murdered by Natives.

Donald Morrison

A Gaelic-speaking gunslinger in Québec? Not a combination most folks would expect to come across, but in the late 1880s and early 1890s, Scot Donald Morrison was one of the most notorious outlaws in Canada.

Morrison was raised in one of the numerous Eastern Townships communities settled by new arrivals to Canada from the Isle of Lewis in the late 1830s. His family arrived in the Lake Megantic area in 1838, and as soon as he was old enough, Morrison left home to work as a cowboy. The work took him as far away as Texas, and he learned to handle a six-shooter pretty well.

Life started to turn sour for Morrison in 1883 when he had to use his $700 in savings to help his parents, who were threatened with eviction from their 200-acre farm. Sadly, his father, Murdo, was becoming senile and not only managed to plunge the farm back into debt but also allowed a crooked Scots moneylender, Major Malcolm McAulay, to swindle him over an $11,000 mortgage. Morrison's troubles worsened when he got bad legal advice and ended up suing his own father and forcing the farm up for auction. Major McAulay outbid Morrison for the farm in 1887 and served an eviction notice on the family.

Morrison refused to leave and had to be evicted by force. He made it clear to everyone in the neighbourhood that anyone who moved onto the family farm would regret it. Most of his fellow Scots knew enough about Morrison to take his warning seriously, but a Canadien family decided to move in. A mysterious stranger with a Scots accent called on the family twice and told them to leave the farm. They ignored the warnings, and shots were fired through the farmhouse window a few weeks later. Then the barn burned down.

Morrison was the obvious suspect, and a warrant was issued for his arrest for attempted murder and fire raising. However, anyone who came looking for Morrison was met by a wall of silence. An amazing number of farmers, both Scot and Canadien, forgot all their English when strangers called. Once, when the police surprised Morrison at an old woman's house, he dived under her bed—leaving his feet sticking out. The woman faced the police officers and began talking in Gaelic, but instead of speaking to the officers, she was telling Morrison to pull his feet in. The police officers, who didn't speak Gaelic, were none the wiser and did not search the woman's home.

When an American called Lucius Warren turned up at the old Morrison place, he boasted that he would take care of the outlaw. McAulay had the American, who claimed to be a gunslinger, sworn in as a special constable. Morrison decided to steer clear of the loud-mouthed American and only went into Megantic when the self-proclaimed gunslinger wasn't around. But one day, Morrison got bad information and came face to face with Warren on the street. The two men argued, and the American went for his gun. Morrison was quicker and put a bullet through Warren's neck. He walked calmly away but returned in disguise a few days later for his would-be killer's funeral.

Most of the locals still sided with Morrison, and they responded to the $2000 reward offered for his capture by setting up a Morrison Defence Organization. They suggested that Morrison should turn himself in and use the reward money to fund his own defence in court. The frustrated authorities increased the reward to $3000 and drafted soldiers, prison guards and American private detectives to hunt the Gaelic outlaw, now dubbed "Canada's Rob Roy" by the press. Anyone suspected of helping Morrison or even being sympathetic to his cause was arrested, and several of his supporters fled into the woods to escape persecution.

A local judge arranged a three-day truce in a bid to cool the tense situation down, but when Morrison took advantage of the truce to visit his parents, the outlaw was ambushed. A gun battle followed, and Morrison was captured after being shot in the hip. He was taken to Sherbrooke for trial.

A fighting fund got Morrison the best lawyers available to defend him against the charge of murdering Warren. Even though the lawyers argued Morrison had acted in self-defence because Warren had gone for his gun first, the jurors found him guilty of manslaughter, but they recommended the lightest sentence possible. The judge sentenced Morrison to 18 years hard labour. Within 18 months, Morrison had lost the will to live and stopped eating. On June 19, 1894, he was sent to the Royal Victoria Hospital in Montréal. He died within hours.

CHAPTER SEVEN

HOW THE SCOTS CREATED CANADA

The birth of a nation can be a long and often dysfunctional process. It can be even tougher when nearly all the fathers of the nation are Scots. For more than 50 years, these men bickered and fought over the future shape of their new home, and some of the scars suffered in those days have never quite healed.

The War of 1812 caused more than physical damage. After the war ended, the heavy hand of political oppression came down hard on any move toward popular democracy because the ruling class regarded it as dangerous pro-American agitation. Many of the actual administrators were English, but they enjoyed the backing of a rich and powerful group of Scottish merchant princes. The Scots with their hands on the levers of power were variously described as the Scotch Faction, the Scotch Party or even The Clan. Together, the Scots merchants and English administrators were known as the Family Compact, which ruled Upper Canada.

Not all Scots supported the merchants, but it took religion to force a revolt. Religion played a far bigger part in Canadian life in the 1800s than it does now. The London-based Parliament was determined that the Church of England—or the Anglican Church, to use its cover name—would rule supreme in Canada. The church was granted control of the education system and one-seventh of the land in the colony, which provided it with an income. It was a wise man who joined the Church of England on arrival in Canada, and Aberdeenshire quarryman's son John Strachan, formerly a member of the Church of Scotland, was nothing if not wise. Strachan became a pillar of the Family Compact. Besides joining the Church of England (he was appointed bishop of Upper Canada in 1839), Strachan also ensured his future advancement in Canada by marrying into the powerful McGill clan of Scottish merchants.

The Church of England in Canada was a greedy and aggressive organization bent on obstructing social progress and restricting educational opportunities for the masses. It demanded a monopoly on solemnizing marriages and held economic development hostage because of its ownership of key plots of land. Restrictions on education and the chance to make a buck were guaranteed to raise the hackles of many Scots, and it wasn't long before Strachan had stirred up trouble with them.

When Robert Gourlay arrived in Canada from Fife in 1817, he quickly realized something rotten was going on in Upper Canada. He declared that the colony was run by "a system of paltry patronage and ruinous favouritism." In yet another attack on the Family Compact, Gourlay noted that for all its members' professed loyalty to king and country, they "had learned to turn a pretty penny in the land of graft." Talk like that was not acceptable to the Family Compact, and Strachan declared Gourlay a "dangerous incidendiary." In 1819, the newcomer was arrested for sedition and deported from Upper Canada as an undesirable alien. (Similar legislation would be used again in the 1920s and 1930s to kick foreign-born labour activists out of Canada.)

Another Scot less than impressed by Strachan and the Scotch Faction's activities was Aberdeen-born John Rae (no relation to the Arctic explorer). He wrote: "We leave our native land to be a British, not an English, Province....But we find a party. A powerful and hereto an all prevailing party, who tell us a very different tale, who tell us we must submit to bear the burden, and wear the badge of inferiority and subjection." Rae became the Canadian spokesman for the Church of Scotland, which offered a perfect vehicle to fight the Family Compact's and the Church of England's domination of public life.

The Scots church demonstrated far more Christian zeal than the Anglicans—in part because the English regarded their church as an instrument of social control rather than religious enlightenment (Karl Marx was living in England when he wrote that religion was the opiate of the masses)—and the Scots' Presbyterian organization was far more accountable than the Church of England's system of appointed bishops.

The Scots' religious zeal was also a handicap. The Church of Scotland was frequently split by questions of doctrine and church government. The Scottish church had begun sending missionaries to Canada, but in one of the earliest examples of Canadian nationalism in English-speaking Canada, the existing Scots Presbyterian congregations made it clear they did not welcome the gesture. When the Church of Scotland tore itself apart in the 1840s, there was no reason for the Canadians to follow suit: they already had the kind of set-up the reformers in Scotland were demanding. But being Scots, and loving a good argument, the Presbyterians in Canada joined the fight between traditionalists and the reformers of the Free Kirk. More Canadian Scots sided with the reformers, and by the time the rift was healed in 1861, the Free Kirkers outnumbered members of the Church of Scotland by 150,000 to 100,000.

The Scots continued fighting for equal treatment, but it took a Scottish nobleman, the Earl of Dalhousie, to begin breaking the Church of England's stranglehold on Upper Canada. As governor of British North America from 1820 to 1828, he divided the Church of England land among the other established denominations. Although Church of England members made up only one-fifth of the population, the church retained two-fifths of the land reserved to provide church income. The rest was shared between the Roman Catholics, the Methodists and the Church of Scotland. The bad feeling and sense of injustice only ended when the church landholdings were abolished altogether in 1854.

By the 1830s, there were growing calls for the 1791 separation of Upper Canada and Lower Canada (now Québec) to be reversed. Many Canadiens feared this would lead to the disappearance of French Canada, with French speakers overwhelmed by the greater number of English speakers in the proposed united colony. Sadly, many of the Scots clergy and their followers had a rabid distrust, even hatred, of the Roman Catholic Church, and this made union even less attractive to Canadiens.

Louis-Joseph Papineau, who enjoyed some support among Scots in Québec, headed opposition to the union. However, many of the Scots, including Kirkcudbright-born printer and publisher John Neilson, drew the line at the kind of violent revolution Papineau began preaching to his Patriote followers. The Scots-born merchant and politician William Scott, in the Patriote heartland of St-Eustache, also sided with Papineau but refused to take up arms. (In spite of that refusal, he was jailed on a treason charge in the aftermath of the Patriote Rebellion of 1837.) Scott was no stranger to violence. During the 1834 election, he had been savagely attacked by a mob of club-wielding fellow Scots who were outraged at his support for the Catholic Papineau.

Open rebellion broke out in November 1837 after a mob of mainly English speakers, tired of what they saw as Canadien disloyalty to the Crown, skirmished with a group of Patriotes. The authorities overreacted and issued an arrest warrant for Papineau and his closest followers. Papineau fled Montréal, and the flag of rebellion was raised in several nearby communities.

By far the most serious threat to British rule came from the rebels who flocked to Saint-Charles and Saint-Eustache. This rebellion marked the first military campaign of Queen Victoria's reign, and the British Army's Royal Scots regiment played a leading, and often bloody, part in driving the rebels out of the two communities. Papineau had failed in his bid to fend off the union and break the power of the Chateau

Clique (the Lower Canada equivalent of the Family Compact), which continued to hold the reins of power in French Canada.

Papineau's rebellion triggered an ill-conceived and badly run rising in Upper Canada against Strachan and the Family Compact. And, of course, it was led by a Scot. William Lyon Mackenzie was a grotesque crab of a man with a bulging forehead and a hot temper. He'd been kicked out of his native Dundee in Scotland as an incorrigible and not always rational trouble-maker. It wasn't long after his arrival in Canada in 1820 that he clashed with Strachan. A largely self-educated shopkeeper who had dabbled in journalism in Scotland, Mackenzie established his own newspaper, the *Colonial Advocate*, to extol the benefits of U.S.-style democracy. The Family Compact did not appreciate his message, but many other people, particularly recent American immigrants, did. Ironically, when Mackenzie was on the verge of bankruptcy in 1826, it was the Family Compact that unwittingly came to his financial rescue. A mob led by the sons of several leading members of the Compact attacked the offices of the *Colonial Advocate* and threw the paper's printing presses into Lake Ontario. Mackenzie was awarded more compensation than the presses were worth and became a rich man.

Mackenzie was elected to the legislature, but his rebel antics got him expelled—five times. Each time he was expelled, he was re-elected. On the first occasion, in 1831, he was escorted back to the legislature by a procession of 134 sleighs led by a bagpiper. In 1834, he became the first mayor of Toronto, but his administration was a disaster. The voters kicked him out a year later. By then, he'd been re-elected to the legislature, but when it was unexpectedly dissolved, he failed to retain his seat.

Instead of blaming his failure on his own political ineptitude, he blamed the system and the Family Compact.

Mackenzie, who proclaimed himself a firm believer in democracy and who had been happy to accept its verdict when he was winning, now decided violent revolution should be the order of the day. When news reached Toronto of the Patriote Rebellion, Mackenzie accelerated his own plans. He copied out the American Declaration of Independence and Canadianized it a bit, then gathered a 700-strong force of mainly American immigrant farm boys at Montgomery's Tavern on December 4, 1837, and prepared to march on Toronto. In imitation of his hero, the first U.S. president, George Washington, he led the revolution from the back of a white farm horse.

The attempted coup was soon in deep, deep trouble. Anthony Anderson, the only experienced soldier to join Mackenzie and his ragtag band, was killed in a skirmish with Family Compact loyalists on the road to Toronto, and it quickly became clear that Mackenzie was unhinged. He was occasionally seen foaming at the mouth. When he set fire to a house, his followers decided to head back to the tavern for a rethink.

Meanwhile, in Toronto, the panic-stricken leaders of the Family Compact were trying to put together an army of their own, and loyalists were arriving by boat from several points along Lake Ontario to join the fight. By December 7, there were about 1000 men under the command of magistrate James FitzGibbon and arch-Tory Allan MacNab, the son of a Scottish soldier, who had instigated one of Mackenzie's numerous expulsions from the legislature. Thanks to some artillery guns, the loyalists had little trouble dispersing the rebels. After the fighting was over, the British lieutenant-governor, Sir Francis Bond Head, appeared and ordered the loyalists to torch not only the tavern but also the nearby home of a widow and her four children. FitzGibbon's protests went unheeded.

Mackenzie fled to the United States dressed as an old woman, though he refused to shave off his side-whiskers to make the disguise effective. A week later, MacNab was laying siege to the hot-tempered rebel and a group of followers after they seized Navy Island near Niagara Falls. MacNab proved disastrous as a commander, but on the night that he was relieved of command, January 13, 1838, Mackenzie and his followers slunk back into U.S. territory.

Earlier, the rebels' supply ship, the *Caroline*, had been seized by a party of loyalists and set on fire as it sat at its dock on the American side of the river. Contrary to lurid U.S. newspaper reports, it did not plunge burning over the falls but sank in the river. Unfortunately, an American crewman was killed in the scuffle that accompanied the seizure of the ship, and two years later Scot Alexander McLeod was accused of his murder. McLeod's arrest in Lewiston, New York, caused an international incident. McLeod was innocent, but that had never stopped American justice (a contradiction in terms if ever there was one) from hanging a person. The U.S. federal and British governments got involved in a bid to prevent mob hysteria in New York from stringing McLeod up. Cooler heads eventually prevailed, and a New York jury agreed that while McLeod had told Canadian authorities the *Caroline* was making a supply run to Navy Island, he had no part in its seizure.

The Mackenzie and Papineau rebellions thrust two men born in Scotland into the limelight, and the men's reactions changed the course of Canadian history. In 1838, a gang of 200 American adventurers and idealists, inspired by Mackenzie's rhetoric and calling themselves the Hunters and Chasers, crossed the St. Lawrence near Prescott to liberate the supposedly oppressed Canadian masses. The Yankees got a less-than-enthusiastic welcome and soon found themselves besieged in a windmill by the very people they thought they were liberating. After five days, the Americans were forced to surrender and were marched into captivity.

Among the men on standby to repel the invaders was a young Glasgow-born militia private and Kingston lawyer John Alexander Macdonald, who had come to Canada with his family when he was five years old. His legal career was checkered up to this point—many people knew him best for a courtroom fist fight he'd had with another lawyer—and he was losing as many cases as he won. But when Macdonald agreed to represent the captured American invaders, he guaranteed himself nationwide celebrity. The lawyer had no legal status at the Americans' court-martial trial and could only whisper questions for them to ask.

Macdonald was particularly impressed by Nils von Schoultz, the Swedish idealist who took command of the Americans after their supposed leaders abandoned them. Schoultz insisted on pleading guilty to all charges and was hanged alongside 10 of his followers. Macdonald prepared the Swede's will but refused payment. Schoultz wrote to his sister, asking her to ensure no one tried to revenge his death. "Let no further blood be shed," he wrote, "and believe me, from what I have seen, all the stories that were told about the sufferings of the Canadian people are untrue." His words went unheeded, and it was fear of American invasion that finally turned British North America into a united Canada.

As a result of the publicity surrounding the court martial of the Americans, Macdonald's legal practice became much more lucrative. He stopped defending criminals and concentrated on commercial law. That brought him into contact with the rich and powerful, and he became heavily involved in Kingston politics on a Conservative or "Tory" ticket. He was elected to Kingston's town council in 1843 and to the legislative assembly of the province of Canada (formed by the union of Upper and Lower Canada) three years later. The British government had decided to divide the seats in the assembly equally between the old provinces, which were now known as Canada West and Canada East, rather than on the basis of population, which would have given Canada West dominance.

Elections in the 1840s were rowdy and often violent affairs. There were no secret ballots. The voters had to gather at the polling place and proclaim their preferred candidate publicly. Intimidation was rife. Greenock-born Dr. William "Tiger" Dunlop was a hero of the War of 1812, and the former army medic needed all his physical courage to get him through the 1841 election in Huron County. His former employers, the land-developing Canada Company, brought in James McGill Strachan, the son of Family Compact stalwart Bishop John Strachan, to oust him from the assembly. Roads were blocked, electors attacked and soldiers had to be rushed to Huron County to quell the violence. Strachan was first declared the winner, but the backwoods doctor was awarded the seat after allegations of electoral fraud were investigated.

Allan MacNab and the Strachans dominated the Tory Party that Macdonald was becoming increasingly involved in. They were fighting a rearguard action to maintain the life of privilege enjoyed by the Family Compact, but Macdonald realized that the inevitable expansion of the voter base as democratic ideals took hold in Canada meant the benefits of the patronage system would have to be spread more widely. With his sharp legal mind, political pragmatism and outward good humour, Macdonald proved to be a master manipulator of men. He was soon the Conservative's main election campaign manager and went out of his way to ensure the men selected to run for office felt they owed him a personal loyalty. Rival candidates for the Conservative nominations were often bought off with government patronage appointments and also made to feel they owed Macdonald something. To the flamboyant and all too frequently inebriated Macdonald, the end always justified the means.

Macdonald knew that a Tory Party tied to the old Family Compact was doomed at the polls, so he began building a coalition of moderate reformers and Canadiens to broaden the party's appeal. By 1856, Macdonald felt he had a strong enough power base within the party to stage a cabinet coup that ousted MacNab. Canadien Étienne Taché became premier, but as deputy premier, master manipulator Macdonald was the real power in the house.

One man who Macdonald's charm could never win over was dour fellow Scot George Brown, though the two did form a brief alliance for the common good to persuade their fellow politicos to agree to Confederation. Brown had come to Canada via New York in 1843 to set up a newspaper supporting the Presbyterian

Free Kirkers. In Canada, Brown expanded his interests beyond the squabbles of the Scottish church, and he became an advocate for political reform. The Free Kirkers' *Banner* newspaper became the *Globe* in 1844 and preached Brown's political gospel of economic independence and political equality with Britain for Canada. The tall, lantern-jawed Scot urged the British colonies of North America, from Newfoundland west to British Columbia, to form a federation to defeat the ambitions of an openly expansionist United States. He also called for representation by population in the legislative assembly. This was something Brown and Macdonald would never agree on. Macdonald wanted to work with the Canadiens of Canada East, but Brown loathed them and believed the constitution gave them an unfair influence over how the colony was run.

However, Brown supported the Rebellion Losses Bill of 1849, which threatened to tear Canada apart. The bill allocated thousands of dollars to compensate people who had lost property during the rebellions of 1837. The problem was that most of the damage had been done in the Montréal area by British soldiers and loyalists. Many Tories felt that the bill failed to distinguish between rebel and loyalist claims for compensation. They objected to the fact that disloyalty to Britain was being rewarded, but the bill was passed by an assembly dominated by an alliance of Reformers and Canadiens. The Tories believed the new governor, the Earl of Elgin, would refuse to ratify the bill and would instead send it to London, where it would be killed off.

But James Bruce, the 8th Earl of Elgin and kinsman of Scottish hero King Robert the Bruce, was a tougher cookie, and he believed more strongly in democracy than the Tories realized. He recognized the bill as a legitimate example of democratic will, and he ratified it. Instead of the law being hailed as a victory for Canadian independence from Britain, though, Elgin's decision sparked a Tory-inspired backlash that saw riots in the streets of Montréal, which was still Canada's biggest city and commercial capital. The wicked MacNab urged his Tories, many of them leading Scottish businessmen, to incite the mobs. "If we don't make a disturbance about this, we shall never get in," he declared. Elgin was pelted with eggs as he left the assembly, and his carriage was pursued through the streets by a rock-throwing mob.

The Tories then organized a mass rally at the Champ de Mars, which, as they knew it would, quickly got out of hand. The mob made its way to the Parliament buildings, where bright lights behind pane glass proved too tempting to excited men with rocks. After smashing the windows, the crowd surged inside and began vandalizing the building. Some began throwing balls of burning paper at each other, and soon fires began breaking out. The magnificent building was engulfed in flames as the mob battled to keep the city's firefighters away. Five days later, as Elgin went to the assembly's temporary home in the city to receive an address of support, his coach was attacked again. Afterward, no fewer than 126 rocks and other missiles were found on the floor of the carriage. There was even talk of assassinating the Scottish nobleman. Two Tory-dominated organizations, St. Andrew's Society of Montréal and the Thistle Curling Club, revoked his honorary presidencies. Elgin, in return, deprived Montréal of the legislative assembly and ordered it to hold its meetings in a rotation between Québec and Toronto.

Besides recognizing Canada's right to make its own decisions by ratifying the Rebellion Losses Act, Elgin also asserted the colony's economic independence by negotiating a free-trade agreement with the United States. The treaty was not renewed after the American Civil War, but loss of trade was not the only concern raised by the end of the war in 1865. The Americans now had the mightiest war machine in the Americas, and its obvious target was British North America. The British had been sympathetic to the rebel South during the war, and a Montréal magistrate's release of some captured Canadian-based Confederate raiders on a legal technicality had caused outrage in Washington. The fact that most Canadians had been in sympathy with the Union states didn't appear to carry much weight with the rabid annexationists in America.

But instead of moving northward after crippling the Confederate states, the Union government discharged its war-weary troops and concentrated its small peacetime army on wiping out the Plains Indians who stood in the way of westward expansion.

One group of Union veterans didn't want to return to civilian life, though. Toward the end of the war, the Union army had recruited new members straight off immigrant ships as they arrived in Boston and New York. Many of the newcomers were young Irishmen fleeing the potato famine that was wreaking havoc in their homeland. When the war ended, they had no homes or jobs to return to and fell easy prey to the Fenian Brotherhood, a group of Irish nationalist extremists and veterans of the American Civil War who saw attacks on Canada as a good way to irritate the British. The Fenian invasions were badly organized, and the raw troops of the Canadian militias managed to push the Irish war veterans back across the border on several occasions. Even if the Canadians did not win a battle outright, they fought the Fenians to a standstill and forced them to retreat as fresh militia troops approached. John A. Macdonald even went so far as to establish a secret service, run by fellow Scot Gilbert McMicken, who reported only to him, to deal with the twin threats of Fenian invasion and American expansionism.

The real solution to the threats, obvious to Macdonald and many other Scottish politicians, was to unite the colonies of British North America to block American military and commercial imperialist ambitions. Canadian unification had been on the political agenda since the 1790s, but it never became an urgent issue until the 1860s. William Lyon Mackenzie had favoured uniting all the colonies, as did George Brown, but there were many Scots who were nervous about the proposed union. They looked at Scotland's shotgun marriage with England in 1707 and were all too aware of the disastrous consequences of a hasty consent.

They had also learned the lessons of 1707, though, and strove to come up with a model of government that was strong but ensured local interests were not sacrificed to appease the self-interests of the biggest partners. What the Scots achieved in Canada in 1867, their cousins in Scotland had to wait another 130 years to realize. Until recently, Scotland basically had a provincial government without a legislature. Ministers were appointed by the central government in London, and decisions affecting only Scots were made by English politicians with no electoral mandate to make them. In the years leading up to 1997, the British Conservative government did not have enough democratically elected Scottish MPs to fill all the ministerial positions at the Scottish Office, as the quasi-colonial administration was known, and had to bring in hereditary noblemen and the British version of Canadian senators from the House of Lords. In 1997 the Scottish Office was finally replaced by a democratically elected assembly. (The Scottish-dominated Liberal Party in Nova Scotia achieved responsible government in 1848—the first instance of responsible government in the British Empire—so it's no wonder that many Scots, such as Beamish Murdoch, Hugh Bell, James McNab and William and George Young, preferred to live there rather than Scotland.)

All the Fathers of Confederation, with the exception of Québec's George-Étienne Cartier and Irishman D'Arcy McGee, were Scots-born or of Scottish descent. The list is long—very long when the Scots who dominated most of the colonial legislatures involved are included—and it's not possible in this book to give them all the individual credit they deserve. But even with the backing of his fellow Scots, Macdonald had his work cut out for him, and there were times when it looked as though the house of cards he was constructing would collapse. He had to stamp out the last vestiges of the old Family Compact if the Tory Party was to become a broad political coalition capable of resolving the regional differences that dogged the process. One of the biggest challenges he faced was convincing the Canadiens in Québec that Confederation would actually strengthen their culture and rights. He had to placate George Brown at the *Globe* and persuade him to convince the Reform Party's Clear Grit members, advocates of U.S.-style democracy, to accept a union based on British principles. Brown did this by, among other things, taking over the two main Grit newspapers, the *Examiner* and the *North American*, and changing their editorial policies so they supported westward expansion for Canada and toed a more pro-British line.

New Brunswick, Prince Edward Island and Nova Scotia were all concerned that they would be swallowed up by Central Canada, and it took a lot of cajoling before they signed on to the deal. New Brunswick and Nova Scotia entered Confederation along with Ontario and Québec in 1867, but Prince Edward Island didn't come on board until 1873. In British Columbia, the Scot-dominated legislature was demanding a transcontinental rail link, thought by many to be beyond Canada's limited financial resources, as the price for joining Canada. Only Newfoundland, where the Scottish influence was tiny if not non-existent, showed no real interest in joining Confederation. (Many Newfoundlanders believe to this day that the 1949 plebiscite, which approved joining Confederation, was rigged by the British, who didn't want them anymore but didn't want the Americans to get them either.)

It looked at one point as though New Brunswick would join the United States instead of Canada, but an ill-advised Fenian raid, a bungled bid to build a railway line across the border, and some much needed cash from Macdonald and Brown that greased the political machine allowed Peter "Bismarck" Mitchell, another Scot, to engineer a pro-Confederation majority in the legislature. After Nova Scotia signed on, a new government led by Joseph Howe, a non-Scot, was elected on an anti-Confederation ticket. Macdonald, Brown and Cartier had some anxious moments before the British government declared it would not support or approve Nova Scotia's quitting Canada. Nova Scotia stayed.

Generally, Macdonald managed to schmooze and charm the delegates at the series of conferences held to discuss Confederation in the same easy way he handled the various factions that made up the Conservative Party. He wrote up most of the draft resolutions for what became the British North America (BNA) Act and ushered in Confederation. The whole process almost came to an abrupt and untimely end when Macdonald accidentally set fire to his hotel room in London just before the British Parliament approved the BNA Act, but Macdonald was rescued by other members of the Canadian delegation.

Not long after the act was approved, Macdonald sent his Turriff-born finance minister, John Rose, to England to act as an unofficial ambassador. Rose was replaced 10 years later by another Scot, Alexander Galt, who became Canada's first High Commissioner in London.

Another move Macdonald made had far more serious and tragic consequences. He bought the Hudson's Bay Company's Rupert's Land territories for the Dominion of Canada, but he failed to take into account the rights of the people, mainly Métis, Native and Inuit, already living there. The Métis of the Red River Colony reacted by forming their own government, led by Louis Riel, and refusing to let Macdonald's governor set foot on the territory without permission. The HBC factor at Red River, William Mactavish, was dying from tuberculosis and would not do anything about Riel, and several Scots at Red River actually gave Riel active support. Orkney man Andrew Bannatyne was even appointed the provisional government's first postmaster. In the end, it took Macdonald's wily Scottish friend Donald Smith, head of the HBC in Montréal, to negotiate terms for the colony's union with Canada and prepare the ground for the bloodless capture of Red River by a column of British and Canadian militia troops under the command of the Perthshire Light Infantry's Garnet Wolseley. When the province of Manitoba was created in 1870, the first meeting of the legislature was held in Bannatyne's home.

The Fenians tried to take advantage of the power vacuum created when Riel left Red River before the arrival of Canadian administrators. They planned an invasion, but the Métis leader sent word from exile in the United States that a force of Métis sharpshooters would be sent to capture the Irish renegades. If the Fenian invasion had been successful, it is possible that Americans would have annexed the whole of western Canada.

Macdonald arranged for a secret payment of $1000 to Riel, on the condition that he stay out of Canada, and Donald Smith came up with another £600 for the Métis leader. However, Riel returned to the country after he was elected to the federal parliament in 1873 and even signed the members' registry in Ottawa, but that was nothing compared to the chaos in 1885 when he became the spiritual leader of another Métis rebellion centred in what would eventually become Saskatchewan. Canadian militia crushed the rebellion, and this time Macdonald showed Riel no mercy. Macdonald caved in to pressure from Protestant extremists in Ontario and vowed, despite an equally vocal pro-Riel outcry in Québec, that the Métis leader would hang. Riel refused to plead insanity at his trial, though such a plea would have been justified, and was found guilty of treason. After he was hanged, lengths of rope allegedly cut from his noose were sent as souvenirs to rabid Protestant Orangemen in Ontario. It has been said that if all those lengths of rope were laid end to end, they would stretch from Toronto to Montréal.

Macdonald had a darker side hidden behind his apparent geniality. He was a binge drinker, as evidenced by his bulbous red nose, and could be a real hater. For example, Macdonald never forgave Donald Smith for voting against him after it was revealed that Scottish millionaire Hugh Allan had made substantial contributions to the Conservative Party during the 1872 federal election in a bid to win the contract to build the transcontinental rail line. However, most people still preferred Macdonald to George Brown. When Brown criticized Macdonald for his drinking, the former lawyer retorted, "I know the electors of Canada would rather have John A. drunk than George Brown sober." Macdonald was right. (Ironically, alcohol became Brown's downfall. He died from blood poisoning in 1880 after being shot and wounded by a *Globe* employee he'd fired for drunkenness.)

Macdonald, best known as "Old Tomorrow" for his ability to put off the really tough decisions, died after a stroke in 1891. Canada and the Conservative Party he created would never see his like again. The Scot who beat Macdonald in the 1873 election, held in the wake of the scandal about Hugh Allan's contributions to the Tories, is often overshadowed by his colourful and charming predecessor as prime minister. Alexander Mackenzie liked plain suits and straight dealing. He even liked being just plain Alexander Mackenzie and refused a knighthood when it was offered. He was an austere man and was one of the many Scottish stonemasons who found a lucrative outlet for his skills in Canada during the construction boom of the 1840s. He was also a friend of George Brown and enjoyed the political support of the *Globe*, known as "the Scotchman's Bible" in western Ontario. Mackenzie continued Canada's drive for economic and political independence and stood for honesty, economy and efficiency in government. Sadly for him, he took power during a worldwide economic slump and was trounced at the polls by that charismatic and likeable rogue Macdonald in 1878.

Those two men, whose respective strengths compensated for the other's weaknesses, laid the foundations between 1867 and 1891 that turned a collection of British colonies into a nation in its own right. In 1899, when the governor general, the Earl of Minto, ordered Canadian troops to South Africa to fight the farmers of the two Boer republics, Prime Minister Sir Wilfrid Laurier countermanded him. Canada did send troops, 7000 of them, to fight in the war, but they went on Canadian terms and not at imperial command. The country built by exiled Scots and their children and grandchildren had come of age.

Canada's Last Duel

There aren't many judges who have stood trial for murder. But in one of his first courtroom appearances, Scots-born John Wilson was in the dock for a murder trial that scandalized Ontario in 1833.

Wilson, who was born in Paisley, was accused of murdering the son of a Scottish army officer in what is believed to be the last duel fought in Canada. Duelling was not the usual way to settle disputes in the Canada of the 1830s, but Wilson and fellow law student Robert Lyon decided to resort to pistols at dawn.

The two friends had fallen out after Lyon said something rude about his fiancée, Elizabeth Hughes, and Wilson, who was in love with Hughes himself, took offence. He confronted Lyon, and Lyon punched Wilson. It wouldn't have been a fair fight because Lyon was a much larger and stronger man, and Wilson let it go.

The matter might have rested there but for the fact that the dispute became the talk of Perth, where the two men were studying. Henry La Lievre, supposedly a friend of Lyon, also had his eye on Elizabeth Hughes and saw the trouble between the two Scots as his chance to move in on her. La Lievre, whose father had fought for the British against his own French people after Napoleon crowned himself emperor of France, stoked the fires and persuaded the law students that this affair of honour could only be settled by a good, old-fashioned duel.

Neither of the Scots was keen on the idea, but La Lievre goaded them with accusations of cowardice, and Wilson reluctantly challenged Lyon to an early morning duel in a farmer's field near the aptly named Scotch Line outside Perth. The pistols used were stolen from a local store. Many people believe neither man loaded his weapon with bullets. The pair fired at each other and when neither was hit, Lyon said he was willing to apologize to Wilson. La Lievre would not hear of a reconciliation and goaded the students to reload. Both made sure there were bullets in the pistols this time, and on an agreed signal they fired again. Lyon threw up his hands and fell to the ground. Wilson's bullet had pierced his heart.

Wilson and his second, fellow Scot Simon Robertson, immediately turned themselves in, but La Lievre went on the run. The young law student put his studies to good use and managed to get himself and Robertson acquitted. Wilson then married Elizabeth Hughes and went on to enjoy a successful career as a Conservative politician and one of the leading lawyers in Ontario, where he was known as "Honest John." Wilson became a judge of the Ontario Court of Common Pleas and was one of the judges who helped try the Fenians who had attempted to invade Canada in the mid-1860s. His death sentences for seven of the raiders led to threats against his life. Wilson responded by touring the northern United States to show he was not afraid of the Fenians and their supporters. However, it is believed that the strain of his involvement in the trials brought on health problems that led to his death in 1869.

JAMES MACLEOD

While the U.S. Cavalry was carrying out a genocidal war against the Plains Indians during the 1870s and '80s, it was a far different story north of the 49th parallel. Much of the credit for that goes to James Macleod, the Scots-born commissioner of the North West Mounted Police.

The federal government in the newly created Dominion of Canada had just bought the territory that would become Saskatchewan and Alberta from the Hudson's Bay Company and could not afford trouble with the Native people. Canada had no real army and certainly couldn't afford the million dollars a head that it's estimated the U.S. Cavalry was spending to kill Natives.

Scottish-born prime minister Sir John A. Macdonald was already thinking of forming a red-coated, paramilitary police force—based on the model of the Royal Irish Constabulary, but mounted—when the Americans forced his hand. Some renegade wolf hunters attacked a peaceful Assiniboine camp in the Cypress Hills because someone had stolen a couple of their horses. The wolf hunters were linked to Fort Whoop-Up, an

American-owned trading post on Canadian territory, where whisky was being bootlegged to local Natives. The Americans' misbehaviour was threatening to start a Native war in Canada, and the Conservative government in Ottawa decided it would be cheaper to hire a police force than fight a war.

Among the first men to be recruited was James Macleod, an Ontario lawyer and militia officer. He'd been born on the Isle of Skye but spent his childhood on a farm north of Toronto. Some say the young Scots boy was befriended by an Ojibwa family, which led to his gaining sympathy and respect for all Natives.

Macleod's father had been a soldier in the British Army, and his service in Central America had left him a sick man. He persuaded his son to go to university and become a lawyer. But Macleod had Highland warrior blood in his veins and soon joined the militia. He fought against the Fenians who staged raids into Canada in the 1860s and distinguished himself during the arduous march by British regulars and Canadian militia to crush the 1870 rebellion at Red River.

Macleod, bored with part-time soldiering and the law, went to Scotland to seek his fortune. But his Conservative credentials meant that when the new North-West Mounted Police (NWMP) force was being formed, he was called back to Canada to be second-in-command. He led the NWMP's first raid on bootleggers near Lake Winnipeg during the famous march west to Fort Whoop-Up. The bootleggers had been tipped off, but they'd left their whisky behind, and Macleod and his men took a dram each to fend off the cold before torching the hooch.

Macleod was one of the best and most sensible officers the new force had, and he proved to be the brains of the operation. The force's first commissioner, George French, trusted Macleod with all the most difficult missions. It was Macleod who was sent to clear out Fort Whoop-Up. It was Macleod who crossed the 49th parallel and travelled to Fort Benton to hunt down the wolf hunters who killed the Assiniboine. He found them easily—the Yanks were boasting openly about killing the thieving, pesky redskins—but a jury of their peers in Helena refused to extradite the seven men to face justice. Instead the jury wanted Macleod charged with false arrest.

Macleod saw another example of how things were done south of the border when he and his men busted five Americans for bootlegging whisky to the Natives. Fort Benton trader "Waxy" Weatherwax paid the $500 in fines Macleod had levied on four of the bootleggers and sprang them from jail. The fifth bootlegger was black. He was left to rot in a Mountie cell but managed to escape a few months later.

Macleod's hard line against the bootleggers won him many friends among the leaders of the local Native communities, who were sickened by the way alcohol was destroying their traditional way of life. Another threat to their way of life was the deliberate destruction of the buffalo herds that moved across the prairies with no regard for international boundaries. Macleod tried without success to introduce conservation measures.

The Scot always tried to be honest and fair in his dealings with the Natives and made it clear that justice was not dispensed on racial lines. A white thief or murderer would receive the same treatment as his Native counterpart. James Macleod soon earned the trust of Blackfoot leader Crowfoot and Blood leader Red Crow, who called him *Stamix Otokan*—Bull's Head. Red Crow declared, "Three years ago when the police first came to this country, I met and shook hands with *Stamix Otokan* at

Pelly River. Since then he has made many promises. He kept them all—not one of them has even been broken. Everything that the police have done has been good. I trust *Stamix Otokan* and will leave everything to him."

When the Sioux in the United States finally massed for war after yet another treaty was broken, they invited the Blackfoot to join them against the whites. Crowfoot went to Macleod and believed him when he said the Sioux had no chance against the military and industrial might of the United States.

Macleod and French, a snobbish Englishman, eventually fell out, and the Scot took on the post of magistrate for the North-West Territories in early 1876. But French's days were numbered. Six months later French was fired by the Liberal government, and Macleod was invited to replace him, despite his links to the Conservatives.

Meanwhile, the Sioux were fleeing an American army bent on revenging the slaughter of the glory-hunting Colonel George Armstrong Custer and his 7th Cavalry troops at Little Big Horn. Macleod met Sioux leader Sitting Bull after he crossed into Canadian territory looking for sanctuary. Macleod tried to broker a deal between the Sioux and U.S. officials, but the talks broke down. Macleod told Sitting Bull that he and his people could remain as long as they obeyed Canada's laws, but they would never get their own reserve or government rations.

Macleod was having enough problems feeding the Canadian Natives, who were facing starvation thanks to the near-extinction of the buffalo. He was also fighting a losing battle against white encroachment on Native land. The new Conservative government under Sir John A. was undercutting the promises Macleod had made to the Natives in good faith. In 1880, Macleod resigned from the Mounties for the second time.

He went back into law, first as a magistrate and then as a Supreme Court judge for the North-West Territories' Judicial District of Southern Alberta. He died of Bright's disease in 1894. Sadly, the good relations he established and fostered between the Natives and the Mounties would not last.

Fort Macleod in southern Alberta is named in his honour, and it was Macleod who gave the city of Calgary its name in tribute to Calgary Bay on the Scottish island of Mull.

Top Cop

While Scot Sir Arthur Conan Doyle was inventing the Victorian super-detective Sherlock Holmes, Canada had its own master sleuth in the form of Scotsman John Wilson Murray. By the time he died in 1906, Murray was acknowledged to be Canada's top cop.

Murray was the son of an Edinburgh sea captain who brought his family to New York around 1845. When his mother Jeanette became sick and returned to Edinburgh, John went with her and was educated at the prestigious Royal High School. Later in life, Murray tended to embroider his life story. He claimed that he ran away from school when he was 13 years old and sailed back to New York. He joined the United States Navy around 1857, and during the American Civil War he served on a Union warship on the Great Lakes. He later claimed he was instrumental in foiling an attempt by Confederate agents based in Canada to free 5000 rebel officers held at a prison camp on Johnson Island in Lake Erie.

Murray joined the Lake Erie police department as a detective in 1868 and was soon investigating a series of arsons in the city. He discovered the fires were being set by firefighters involved in a feud over who the new fire chief should be. The detective's suspicions were aroused because the fire department's pumper trucks started arriving before anyone had spotted the blazes.

Murray was then hired as a detective by the Canadian Southern Railway, which suspected that the rival Great Western Railway was trying to derail its trains. In 1875, the railroad job led to an offer to become the Ontario government's one and only full-time detective. Up until then, private detectives had been hired for specific cases. Murray's work took him all over Ontario. It wasn't until 1884 that he was given an assistant.

Murray soon earned the nickname "Old Never-let-go" for his dogged and tireless pursuit of criminals. He was a pioneer of crime-scene investigations and would spend days crawling on his hands and knees, painstakingly looking for clues in the area where a body had been found. Victims' bodies were often buried before Murray arrived in the pioneer farming communities of rural Ontario, and he would always have the remains dug up for an autopsy. He was able to prove that a man who friends claimed had been killed by a falling tree had in fact been hit over the head with an axe.

Some of his methods were unorthodox. In his most famous case, the body of a man was found in a swamp with two bullet holes in the back of his head. Murray sat the corpse in a chair and contemplated it for several minutes. When he asked the corpse who the killer was, the body slumped to the ground. Though all identifying labels had been cut from the man's suit and underwear, Murray believed the clothing was English. He had a photograph taken of the dead man and circulated it to newspapers in Canada, the United States and Britain.

The killer himself answered the appeal for information regarding the photograph, and the dogged Scot demolished his alibi piece by piece. It turned out the victim was a young Englishman who answered a newspaper advertisement offering a farm partnership in Ontario. Wilson had no doubt that the killer had been planning to murder anyone who was lured to Canada by the advert. The big break in the case came when a second Englishman came forward and said the killer had twice tried to push him over the cliffs at Niagara shortly after he arrived to check out the farm.

Murray also made use of bloodstain analysis and fingerprints to catch criminals. He once cut a piece of turf from a murder scene because it had a footprint in it. He then matched the print with his prime suspect's footwear. Some of his methods would be frowned on by the justice system today. For one case, he sneaked into a barbershop and shaved off part of a suspect's beard to find a distinctive zigzag scar that confirmed his identity. He'd need a search warrant to do that these days. In another case, Murray suspected a farmer of burning down four barns in the area, including his own, and blaming the fires on the local black community. Murray tricked the suspect into leaving his farmhouse unattended and then searched the house to find examples of the man's handwriting. The writing matched that on the notes left at the four fire scenes warning "white trash" not to insult "our coloured folks." Nowadays, an illegal search like that would not be admitted as evidence. (It's interesting to note that the motive in this case was not racial, but insurance fraud.)

Another well-known case involved a family of American forgers who flooded Canada with more than $1 million worth of counterfeit bills—a lot of money in the 1880s.

The father was a master engraver who taught his sons how to make counterfeit banknote printing plates and taught his daughters how to forge the bank officials' signatures on the notes. The first clue that a counterfeiting ring was operating was that the fake bills were of far better quality than the real ones.

Not all cases were so serious. Murray caught two brothers who were offering high school kids a chance to see their final exams before they sat for the test—for a fee. Murray was soon inundated with complaints from people who claimed to have paid for the exam papers to "keep them out of the wrong hands." Murray wrote the brothers, posing as a young girl who wanted to make sure she passed her high school exam so she would get into university. He then waited for the brothers to arrive at the post office to pick up the latest crop of replies and nabbed them.

Murray was involved in 19 murder cases during his 30-year career as Ontario's most senior detective. When he died in 1906, the *Toronto Daily Mail and Empire* declared he had been "intimately associated with the prosecution of nearly every criminal case of importance in the province outside of the larger cities."

TOMMY DOUGLAS

The Scots' contribution to political life in Canada didn't end with Confederation, but it did start to slow down a bit. In 1910, however, a young immigrant boy arrived who would dramatically change life in Canada and the way Canadians see themselves. Little Thomas Clement Douglas grew into a giant in Canadian politics.

It wasn't so much what Douglas did as what he made other politicians do. The federal Liberals are notorious for stealing other people's ideas and making them their own, and that's what they did with Douglas's ideas. They actually offered him a job with their party, but he turned it down because he believed it would cramp his style. In a television interview years later, he explained why he rejected Liberal prime minister Mackenzie King's offer shortly before World War II. "I'm not interested in getting power unless you can do something with this power," he told the interviewer. "I have watched politicians for the last 40 years drop their principles to get power, only to find those who controlled the party that they joined prevented them from doing all the things they really believed in." And in the end, Douglas probably didn't even care who improved the lives of everyday Canadians as long as their lives were improved.

Douglas was born in the Scottish town of Falkirk in 1904. It's not clear just how and when he decided to become a social crusader. It may have been when, as a child in Winnipeg, Douglas injured his knee and contracted a bone infection. His family couldn't afford proper treatment, and the leg would have been amputated if a surgeon hadn't offered to treat him if he would agree to be a teaching subject for the surgeon's medical students. Others say he decided to push a program of universal health care because during his days as a young Baptist preacher, two of his parishioners died because they could not afford medical attention.

In Douglas's day, politics and religion did mix. The family pastor in Winnipeg was Co-operative Commonwealth Federation (CCF) founder J.S. Woodsworth. Douglas was working his paper route one day when he saw Woodsworth arrested and two men killed after the RCMP opened fire on striking workers in Winnipeg in June 1919.

As a teenager, Douglas had been offered the chance to attend drama school, but he decided he preferred saying his own words to reciting someone else's. In 1924, he enrolled at the Baptist-run Brandon College and became interested in the possibilities offered by preaching the "social gospel," which applies Christian principles to alleviate social problems. Brandon College was attractive to a poor, working-class boy because its tuition costs were low. Another incentive for Douglas was that the college was willing to let him take six years to do the three-year course. This was necessary because he had worked a number of jobs to help his parents pay the family's bills, which meant his education had been erratic.

In 1931, he was ordained as a Baptist minister. He was able to use the little tricks he'd picked up as a child actor to enthrall his first congregation in Weyburn, Saskatchewan, with his message of active Christian social reform. Three years later, he decided he could best serve by entering politics, but he was defeated when he stood as a Farmer-Labour candidate in the provincial election. Church leaders told him to keep out of politics, but he ignored them and the following year was elected CCF MP for Weyburn in the federal election. It was his rousing speeches in the House of Commons that prompted William Lyon Mackenzie King, grandson of 1837 rabble-rouser William Lyon Mackenzie, to offer him a job with the Liberal Party.

When World War II broke out, Douglas volunteered for the Winnipeg Grenadiers and would have gone with them to Hong Kong if doctors had not discovered a medical problem with one of his feet. How different Canada might be today if Douglas had been killed by the Japanese or reduced to a human wreck by four years of cruel captivity in a prisoner of war camp, as many of the Grenadiers were.

In 1944, Douglas switched from federal politics to lead the Saskatchewan CCF to a landslide victory. He immediately launched a campaign of social reform that saw isolated farms and villages across Saskatchewan hooked up to a publicly owned electricity grid, allowed public servants to join unions, outlawed sex and race discrimination, and created Canada's first publicly owned automobile insurance agency. His government was also able to eliminate Saskatchewan's $20 million debt thanks to careful management by provincial treasurer Clarence Fines.

Creating a provincial budget surplus allowed Douglas to implement his plan for universal health care. One of the first things he had done in 1944 was make health and dental care free for pensioners. Treatments for cancer, mental illness and tuberculosis were made free to all shortly afterward, and in 1947 the provincial government put in place free hospital care for all—well, free except for a one-time charge of five dollars per person.

When the New Democratic Party (NDP) expanded the plan again to provide universal health care, it met with bitter opposition from many of the province's doctors, who appeared to be businessmen before healers, and they went on strike in 1962 to protest. By then, Douglas had become the first leader of the federal NDP, but his successor in Saskatchewan, Woodrow Lloyd, weathered the strike. Inspired by the Saskatchewan example, the federal Liberal government implemented medicare nationwide in 1968.

The doctors were wrong about medicare. Their average income went up $3000 a year after it was introduced. But Douglas wasn't always right. As a student he had flirted with the idea of compulsory sterilization of the mentally retarded. However, Douglas dropped the scheme and revoked Saskatchewan's eugenics law when he became premier. (A similar law in Alberta was not revoked until 1971.)

As leader of the federal NDP, Douglas did not have the same impact that he'd had in Saskatchewan. After Douglas introduced such a wide-reaching social reform program without bankrupting Saskatchewan, many political leaders at the provincial and federal levels were already introducing similar measures.

Douglas made himself unpopular when he criticized Pierre Trudeau for implementing the War Measures Act in 1970 to deal with a series of bombings and kidnappings by Québec extremists. Douglas argued that the act, which allowed 465 people to be arrested without charge, was a "sledge hammer to crack a peanut."

He gave up the leadership of the NDP in 1971 but stayed on as energy critic until he retired from politics eight years later. He died of cancer in 1986.

CHAPTER EIGHT

TARTAN RIBBONS

Without the transcontinental railroad, there would be no Canada as we know it today. British Columbia would almost certainly be an American state, and the Prairie provinces would either be deserted or another state in the union. And those ribbons of steel would not exist without the Scots.

The railways came to North America in a really big way between the 1850s and World War I, about the same time the Scottish influence on Canada was at its peak. Even then, the Scots never made up more than 15 percent of the population, but they dominated politics, business, finance and education. Building a transcontinental railroad was one of the Scots' greatest contributions. It was a massive undertaking—a line across Canada was 2500 miles long. That was twice as long as the Union Pacific south of the

49th parallel, and this country's geography presented far greater challenges to the Canadian engineers and construction crews.

Only the Scots could have pushed the project through. They had the money, political contacts, business savvy and guts to keep going with the greatest nation-building project when all it seemed to offer them was personal ruin. The railroad was all about networking, from both a transportation point of view and a business one. Networking was something the Scots business community in Canada excelled at, especially as so many of its members were blood relations. Donald Smith of the Hudson's Bay Company and George Stephen, the head of the Bank of Montreal—two men who perhaps did the most to ensure the Canadian Pacific Railway was a success—were cousins born in northeastern Scotland. Both would become lords of the realm and very rich men thanks to the railroad that, in its early days, was constantly threatening to bankrupt them.

Scots had been in the Canadian transport business long before the coming of the railroads. One of the biggest ship operators on the Great Lakes before the War of 1812 was a Scot, Robert Hamilton. The canal systems in Ontario and Québec also owed much to the work of Scots, such as Robert Drummond and William Lauder, who were heavily involved in building the Rideau and Chambly canals in the early 1800s. But the big money in transportation started coming in when the railroads arrived. They were the 19th-century equivalent of today's oil industry or the dot.com companies. Fortunes were there to be made—and lost.

Running a railway line across the rocky, muskeg-dotted landscape north of Lake Superior, which many engineers said was almost impossible, and over the "empty" prairies before scaling the mighty Rockies was not an obvious money maker. But a rail link with eastern Canada was the price British Columbia demanded for joining Confederation in 1871. Three years later, when there was still no sign of the promised railroad, around 800 angry British Columbians stormed the legislature in Victoria. It was obvious to Prime Minister Sir John A. Macdonald that he had to make good on the railroad promise or Canada would begin falling into the hands of the United States, piece by piece.

There was no shortage of men, especially Scotsmen, in Canada with some railroad experience. Even George Simpson of the Hudson's Bay Company had begun investing in the rail lines that were starting to criss-cross eastern Canada from the 1850s onward. Macdonald could have turned to any of several fellow Scots, including George Laidlaw, Alexander Galt, John Torrance, Angus Morrison, Edward McGillivray, Duncan McCrae and David Macpherson, for help with his railroad project. But the Glasgow-born Macdonald turned to the big daddy of them all, shipping millionaire and industrialist Hugh Allan, one of the richest men in Canada and possibly one of the richest Scots in the world at the time.

Allan, in turn, tried to enlist recently appointed senator David Macpherson to join his transcontinental rail scheme, but the former Inverness Academy student was worried about his fellow Scot's ties to U.S. promoters. Macpherson turned Allan down and actually set up a rival rail company, the Interoceanic Railway, to bid for the federal government contract to build the line. Macdonald tried hard to reconcile the pair, but their stubborn Scots pride made this impossible.

Macdonald was also concerned about Allan's links to U.S. railway interests, including Jay Cooke of the Union Pacific, and urged him to ease away from the Americans. Macdonald saw the railroad as an "Imperial Highway" that was intended to keep the Americans out of Canada, not a Trojan Horse that would allow them to slip in and take over Canadian industry.

Macdonald had to fight an election before the railroad contract was awarded to Allan. He won it, but his new government was in a shaky state, and Allan's American partners reacted to Macdonald's attempts to sideline them by destroying the government. Macdonald's Conservatives had begged Allan for financial support during the campaign, and he had responded by funnelling $350,000 to the party. The Americans leaked details of the contributions, the government fell and the Liberals were swept into power in 1873. The American ploy backfired, however, because the Liberals under Alexander Mackenzie cancelled the contract and sent Allan, and the Americans, packing. Mackenzie, unlike Macdonald, didn't owe $80,000 to a bank owned by Allan.

Mackenzie's government tried to have the railroad built piecemeal, one small section after another, but five years later there were only a few hundred miles of isolated track in the wilderness to show for the effort. In the 1878 election, Macdonald and the Conservatives formed the government again after a campaign that promised high import tariffs to protect Canadian industry from American competition, fair and otherwise. Once back in power, Macdonald turned once more to his fellow Scots to build the ribbon of steel he regarded as so vital to Canada's survival. Both he and his Scottish backers were keen to see the wealth of western Canada, the "last best west," exploited by Montréal and Toronto rather than the hated Yankees.

Enter Donald Smith, George Stephen and James Hill, a Canadian with at least one Scottish parent, who had made their fortunes in the railway business south of the border in what became known as the St. Paul, Minneapolis and Manitoba Railway. The partners were interested in building and operating the Canadian transcontinental line, but there was a problem. Macdonald hated Smith with a loathing that burned deep in his soul. He and Smith had once been friends. Macdonald had even sent Smith to Red River in 1869 to deal with Louis Riel and his Métis government, but it was the former fur trader's vote that had proved crucial in bringing down the Tory government in 1873. Macdonald never forgot or forgave. "I'll lick him faster than Hell scorches a feather," snarled Macdonald as colleagues held him back after he attempted to attack Smith in the House of Commons.

Smith was kept well in the background of the deal when the CPR syndicate applied for the rail contract— and the subsidy of $25 million and 25 million acres of free land that went with it. Macdonald must have known about Smith's involvement, but he was prepared to ignore it, as long as it wasn't rubbed in his face, because Smith was a key player in making the dream railroad a reality.

The front man for the syndicate was George Stephen. Like his cousin, Stephen had come to Canada with only a letter of introduction in his pocket, some relatives who could help him find a job and a burning

urge to succeed in the New World. The cousins ultimately became two of the richest men in the British
Empire.

Donald Smith, whose uncle was John Stuart, explorer
Simon Fraser's right-hand man, arrived in Canada in
1838 from his native Forres to work for the HBC. He
proved to be a sharp financial operator (too sharp for
some, who questioned his bookkeeping) and within 10
years was one of the HBC's top fur traders in Labrador. He invested his earnings in the stock market and
in the HBC itself. The Scot's skill as a canny investor
attracted the attention of several of his fellow fur
traders, and soon he was playing the markets with
their money as well. Smith operated a primitive mutual
fund scheme that paid investors fixed interest of 3 percent while he pocketed the rest of the profit. When he
was almost 50 years old, he finally emerged from the
wilds of Labrador and plunged into the world of really
high finance in Montréal.

Stephen and Smith didn't meet until 1865. Stephen
had been a draper's apprentice in Scotland and came
to Montréal to work in a relative's store. He soon
owned the store and diversified into manufacturing
clothing. Smith began helping Stephen sell his woolen
goods to the HBC, and the cousins discovered that,
between them, they owned enough stock in the Bank
of Montreal to control it. In 1872, the pair even went
into business with Hugh Allan, building rolling stock
for the new railroads that were springing up all over
eastern Canada. Stephen had already partnered with
Allan in the Detroit River Tunnel Company.

Another of the cousins' business partners was Richard Angus, who came in for a slice of the action when
they built a railroad linking Manitoba and Minnesota.

Angus, from Bathgate, near Edinburgh, was plucked from the Bank of Montreal to run the railroad. Railroads and real estate speculation went hand in hand, and Smith had been put in charge of the HBC's land sales division. Nothing pushed up property prices like a rail link, and the big money in railroads came from shipping settlers into a virgin area, supplying them with their wants and transporting the fruits of their labours back east.

It was through his efforts to promote transportation links between Red River settlements and the outside world that Smith got to know the one-eyed Hill, a prime mover in the Red River Transportation Company's river steamer service. The pair decided to bring Stephen and Hill's Québec-born business partner Norman Kittson in on an 1878 takeover of the bankrupt St. Paul and Pacific Railroad. The quartet then linked the American line to the Manitoba Western Railway, which Smith had helped incorporate in 1875, to create the St. Paul, Minneapolis and Manitoba Railway Company. Hill, Angus, Smith and Stephen made such a big profit from the line that they decided to go for the Big One—the Canadian transcontinental railroad. There would be no more fumbling in the Arctic, looking for a sea route from the Atlantic to the Pacific via the Northwest Passage. Now goods and people would travel from one ocean to the other by rail.

The four men brought in another of Hugh Allan's former colleagues, Duncan McIntyre. (There would have been few Scots in Montréal at the time who hadn't been in partnership with Allan in some venture.) McIntyre's family had left Perthshire when he was 15 years old to open a store in Renfrew, Ontario. The ambitious young Scot was soon at the helm of the family business and extended its reach into the Eastern Townships, up the Ottawa Valley and along the St. Lawrence. Transportation was obviously a key to business success, and McIntyre began investing in the Canada Central Railway and the Brockville and Ottawa Railway. The Canada Central line was a gold mine as it hauled out the lumber cut in the Ottawa Valley. It was also key to Allan's plans for a transcontinental line because it linked Ontario and Québec. Allan had started buying stock in the Canada Central line, but he lost interest when his plan for the Pacific link collapsed with Macdonald's government in 1873. McIntyre somehow shrugged off his ties to Allan and even managed to get a contract from Mackenzie's Liberals to build a rail line in the Georgian Bay area— but only after he'd engineered Allan's ousting from the board at Canada Central.

McIntyre was appointed Stephen's deputy at Canadian Pacific when the company was formed in 1881, but he resigned in 1884 when it threatened yet again to go bankrupt and take his personal fortune with it. The parting was far from friendly, and McIntyre sued the railroad for debts owing to his stores for supplies. Stephen paid up but refused to be in the same room as McIntyre ever again. The banker wrote to Macdonald that McIntyre was "coarsely selfish and cowardly all through these five years, ruthless in regarding the interests of others when he can advance his own." Stephen added that "when McIntyre deserted the Company he made up his mind that it would burst and that Smith and I would lose every dollar we had in the collapse."

McIntyre wasn't the only one who thought the cousins and other shareholders in the railroad would end up in the poorhouse. James Hill also quit as general manager, and William Van Horne, another railroad expert from south of the 49th parallel, was promoted to replace him. Hill was certain that the financial house of cards, a bewildering series of stock transfers, options and rollovers that Stephen had constructed to keep the Canadian Pacific alive in the face of skyrocketing construction costs, must collapse.

The main construction contractors, mostly Americans, seemed almost completely incapable of laying track on budget. Theft of construction supplies was rampant, and the closer to bankruptcy the CPR rolled, the more the contractors siphoned off to protect what they saw as their own financial interests. The syndicate stumbled from one financial crisis to another. The Grand Trunk Railway in eastern Canada saw the CPR as a direct competitor and was doing everything it could to sabotage its financing arrangements. The Hudson's Bay Company, which was also in the land sales business, obstructed the railroad construction at every turn. Smith was accused of trying to ruin his former employer's reputation in a bid to drive down its stock price so he could gain control of the HBC cheaply. By 1889, Smith *was* the biggest shareholder in the HBC, but that was after the Canadian Pacific line was completed and the profits had finally started to roll in.

The job of fighting the Grand Trunk's efforts to discourage British investment in Canadian Pacific was assigned to another member of the founding syndicate, Aberdeenshire-born lawyer and financier John Rose. He lived to see the railroad profits start to come in, but died in Scotland in 1888 from a heart attack brought on by shooting a stag during a hunting trip.

While Stephen was performing financial miracles to keep Canadian Pacific going, Smith was gaining control of the eastern railroads needed to carry the line to the Atlantic. One by one the Toronto, Grey and Bruce; Credit Valley; Ontario and Quebec; and New Brunswick railroads all came into Smith's financial empire.

The syndicate had agreed to a smaller subsidy and land grant than Allan had negotiated, but by 1883 it was begging for a $22.5-million bailout from the federal government to finish the line. Even with a federal loan, it was touch and go whether they could successfully complete the project. Both Stephen and Smith had to put up their homes as security for loans and dip into their personal bank accounts to meet the payroll for the construction gangs. Disaster was looming by 1885, and it looked as though the syndicate's money was finally gone.

It was Smith's old sparring partner from the Red River who inadvertently saved the CPR. Louis Riel had returned from exile in the United States to become the leader of a Métis uprising at Batoche in the North-West Territories. The federal government responded by sending 3000 militia to crush the Métis and their Aboriginal allies. Van Horne saw his chance to promote the railroad's importance to national security and promised to get the soldiers to Winnipeg within 11 days. The line across the top of Lake Superior was still not complete, but temporary track was laid across the ice, and where the ice on the lake was too thin, sleds were provided. What had seemed impossible—getting Macdonald to squeeze more money out of the government—was possible, and another $5 million was approved. It was enough.

Smith was given the honour of hammering home the "Last Spike" at Craigellachie in the Monashee Mountains on November 7, 1885. He hit the spike with a glancing blow and bent it. Van Horne produced a second spike, which Smith banged in, but it seems fitting that the first Last Spike was crooked.

Sir John A. Macdonald was given a luxury railroad car by a grateful Canadian Pacific.

Once the line was completed, the money rolled in. Smith, Stephen and Van Horne bought and sold real estate in Vancouver on a large scale. Telegraph lines and lines for that newfangled invention the telephone soon ran alongside the rails, and members of the syndicate invested heavily in such companies as Federal Telephone and the Bell Telephone Company of Canada. Smith and Stephen bought stock in the Lake of the Woods Milling Company, which processed western grain for shipment east. They also had stock in the Canadian Salt Company, and the influx of settlers into the west via the railroad made their investment in the North-West Land Company very lucrative indeed. Smith was a founder of Dominion Coal, and he even spotted the potential of the oil industry, becoming one of the founders of the Anglo-Persian Oil Company. Now under the name British Petroleum, Anglo-Persian Oil is one of the four biggest oil companies in the world.

Although he'd left the syndicate a year before the line was completed, Duncan McIntyre profited from the rail boom. He helped found the Bell Telephone Company of Canada and invested in the North-West Land Company and Canadian Light and Power. His ability to be in the right place at the right time with the right amount of money led to his being dubbed the "Canadian Napoleon of finance."

Richard Angus also did well from his investment in the syndicate. He joined Smith and Stephen in buying the Canadian Salt Company and the North-West Land Company. His empire also included the Laurentide Paper Company, the Dominion Coal Company, Dominion Iron and Steel, the Royal Trust Company, the Grand Falls Power Company, the Pacific Power Company, and the London and Lancashire Assurance Company.

Millionaires in those days liked to have the media onside, and the best way to ensure compliance was to own it. Hugh Allan controlled the *Montreal Gazette*, and Smith made an unsuccessful attempt to buy Toronto's *Globe*, which had been critical of the CPR. Smith had more luck silencing his critics in the west when the owner of the *Manitoba Free Press* foolishly accepted a loan from him. The owner couldn't repay the loan, so Smith took control and installed one of Canadian Pacific's publicity men as editor.

Canadian Pacific, bailed out by the taxpayer, made a lot of men—a lot of Scots—rich. But not all the Scots involved in the company were money men juggling stocks in the boardrooms of Montréal, New York and London. Scots, known or nameless, had been preparing the ground for the railway for years. For example, Kicking Horse Pass in the Rockies was named after Edinburgh geologist James Hector, who almost died there after he was kicked by a horse in 1858. Thousands more Scots worked on CPR construction. The job a man got on the construction gangs was often linked to where in the world he came from. Scots tended to be hired as foremen or blasters (working with explosives). They also handled a lot of the engineering work, and several were lead contractors in their own right.

As the original American contractors were pushed aside, Scots with experience building railroads in eastern Canada stepped up to replace them on the toughest jobs. One of the most difficult was the task of laying track along the north shore of Lake Superior. The stretch was described as "two hundred miles of engineering impossibilities." But the Scots' determination and imagination made it possible—though at a higher cost than first budgeted. The only alternative would have been to lay the track on the south shore of the lake, but Macdonald would not allow that because it would have required the line to run through the U.S.

Scot John Ross was brought in to lay the track west of McKay's Harbour on Superior's north shore. He never enjoyed Van Horne's full confidence but did well enough to have McKay's Harbour renamed Rossport in his honour. The section of track required numerous tunnels and bridges; by the time it was completed it was the most expensive stretch of a railroad in North America. One mile-long portion cost $700,000 in 1885 dollars.

Ross relied heavily on the bridge-building expertise of fellow Scot Robert Reid from Coupar. Reid cut his teeth building railroad bridges in eastern Canada before moving to the United States, where he earned the admiration of his fellow engineers by bridging the Colorado River and the Rio Grande. After the Canadian Pacific was built, Reid went on to build a railroad across Newfoundland.

Another Scot brought in to tackle a major headache for Canadian Pacific was James Ross, a former student of the Inverness Academy, like David Macpherson. James Ross was put in charge of pushing the line west from Calgary over the Rockies to meet the Chinese construction gangs working their way east from Port Moody in BC. Ross was prepared to stand up to Van Horne, and the two men had great respect for each other. The stubborn Van Horne usually got his way in the end, but not always. Ross brought in many of the men he had worked with on the earlier Credit Valley and Victoria railroads to build the line across the mountains.

After the Canadian Pacific was finished, Ross teamed up with William Mackenzie and Donald Mann, two Ontarians of Scottish descent who had made their reputations on the CPR, for some of their railroad projects in western Canada. Mackenzie and Mann's network of western Canadian railroads is now known as Canadian National. Ross also joined Van Horne and Stephen in their venture at the Lake of the Woods Milling Company. Ross, Mackenzie, Mann and Van Horne then went into the electric streetcar business. When they ran out of Canadian cities in which to lay tracks, they started building streetcar systems in the Caribbean and Central and South America. The power stations that generated electricity for the streetcars were also used to provide light and meet domestic demand in cities throughout the western hemisphere. Their most successful venture proved to be the Brazilian Traction, Light and Power Company, now known as Brascan.

The construction of the Canadian Pacific picked up where the fur trade left off as the engine driving the Canadian economy. And as with the fur trade, it was Scots who were in the driver's seat.

Scottish Railways

The number of competing businesses in a market is often an indication of big profit potential. What's true for pizza delivery today was true for railroads in the mid- to late 1800s. The following railway companies had strong Scottish connections.

Calgary and Edmonton Railway

Champlain and St. Lawrence Railroad

Coburg, Peterborough and Mamora Railway and
  Mining Company

Eastern Railway

Grand Junction Railway

Grand Trunk Railway

Great Western Railway

Kingston and Pembroke Railway

Lake Manitoba Railway and Canal Company

Manitoba and Southeastern Railway

Manitoba Junction Railway

Montréal and Kingston Railway

Montréal and Lachine Railroad

Montréal Northern Colonization Railway

North Shore Railway

Northern and Western Railway

Ontario, Simcoe and Huron Union Railway

Québec, Montréal, Ottawa and Occidental Railway

St. Lawrence and Atlantic Railroad

Toronto and Guelph Railway

Toronto and Nipissing Railway

Winnipeg and Hudson Bay Railway

Woodstock and Lake Erie Railway and Harbour
  Company

FANTASTIC FLEMING

Scot Sandford Fleming was crucial in mapping out Canada's future—literally.

The Fife carpenter's son had not been in Canada long before he had mapped Toronto harbour, the city itself, Peterborough, Hamilton and Cobourg. In the 1870s, he took on one of the biggest surveying jobs in Canada at the time, proposing the route for the rail link from the Great Lakes to the Pacific. Not bad for a young man who only went as far as Grade Six at the school in his native Kirkcaldy.

Fleming had come to Canada in 1845 with his brother David and cousin Henry Fleming. The Atlantic crossing had been a nightmare, and when they were caught in a particularly violent storm, the young Scots surveyor put a farewell message to his parents in a bottle and threw it overboard. The bottle was found on a beach in southern England, and Fleming kept the letter in the top drawer of his office desk for the rest of his life.

The big money in Canada in the 1850s was to be made from railroads, and Fleming was soon involved in survey work for the Ontario, Simcoe and Huron Railway. He also found time to design Canada's first postage stamp, bearing an engraving of a beaver, in 1851. By 1862, Fleming was convinced that a railway line to the Pacific was not only essential to Canada's future but also a practical proposition. At the time, he was busy working as lead surveyor on the Intercolonial Railway, which was built to link Québec and Halifax, and it wasn't until 1871 that he headed west to find a route for the railroad to the Pacific.

The western journey and survey turned into an epic task involving 800 men fighting their way through muskeg and nearly impenetrable forest and across desolate rock plains and raging rivers. The survey teams alternately faced freezing temperatures or soaring heat, as well as bloodsucking clouds of blackflies and mosquitoes. They covered 5000 miles in 103 days.

The route Fleming chose took the line northwest across the Prairies from Winnipeg to Edmonton and then through the Yellowhead Pass before turning southwest through the Interior to Vancouver. However, the CPR ultimately decided to forestall competition from American railroads by running the line closer to the 49th parallel—from Winnipeg to Calgary instead of Edmonton.

Fleming was the chief engineer on the project from 1871 until 1880, when he was fired by the federal government because of personality clashes. In exchange for going quietly, Fleming was promised the contract for the undersea telegraph cable linking Canada and Australia that he had proposed. (This promise was later broken, though the line was completed in 1902.)

When the Canadian Pacific syndicate got the government contract to build the railway, Fleming was brought back on board and supervised the search for a pass through the Rockies that would carry the line from Calgary to the Pacific. The crucial passes were found, and Fleming was there when Lord Strathcona hammered in the Last Spike at Craigellachie. He's the tall guy with the white beard standing behind Strathcona in the famous photograph.

Fleming also found time to persuade an international committee to accept his plan to divide the world into 24 standard time zones. Up to then, each town set its own clocks. That meant towns only 40 miles apart could be running on different times.

He also tried, unsuccessfully, to persuade the French to make the length of a metre 40 inches instead of 39.37 inches in an effort to make conversion between the two systems of measurement easier.

When Fleming received a knighthood in 1897, it was not for his work on stamps, time or the railroads. Rather, it was for his work promoting the Pacific telegraph cable.

SCOTTISH GIANTS

Canada is a big country, and the Scots provided two of the world's tallest people to live in it.

Most parents of a growing teenage boy will sympathize with the Cape Breton parents of young Angus MacAskill, who had an adolescent growth spurt of epic proportions in the late 1830s. He went from being an average-sized 13-year-old to a height of seven feet, nine inches. His parents literally had to raise the roof of the family home to accommodate him.

MacAskill was a true giant and perfectly healthy. In a tough pioneer community where feats of strength were much admired, the young Scot, born on the island of Berneray in the Outer Hebrides, gave the folks of Englishtown plenty to talk about. He could carry two 300-pound barrels under his arms, shoulder a 60-foot beam and lift grindstones as if they were pillows. MacAskill soon recognized that there might be money to be made from his demonstrations of physical prowess, so when times got hard in Englishtown around 1848, he toured Canada and the United States with a circus. Later he toured the West Indies, Britain and Cuba, and by 1854 MacAskill had earned enough money to buy a store in Englishtown and settle down as a small-business man with farms and a grist mill in nearby St. Ann's. One of his favourite tricks as a storekeeper was to offer to sell people tea for a certain price by either the pound or the fist. Because his hands were so large (the palms measured 8 inches by 12 inches), the latter quantity was the better deal. MacAskill died in 1863 from what doctors at the time called "brain fever."

Nova Scotia was also the home of giantess Anna Bates. Unlike MacAskill, she was a big 'un from the start, weighing 18 pounds at birth. The family of her mother, Ann Graham, came from the Orkney Islands, while her father, Alexander Swan, was from Dumfries. Both were average height, and so were the couple's 12 other children.

Anna was 27 inches long when she was born in 1846, and by the time she was four she was four foot six. At the age of six she was the same height as her mother, five foot two, and when she was 15 she was over seven feet tall. American circus promoter P.T. Barnum signed her up in 1863, when she was seven feet, five-and-a-half inches tall, and took her to New York. When Barnum's museum and freak show on Broadway caught fire, the Scot was trapped inside on the third floor. She could not get down the blazing stairways of the building, and at 400 pounds she was too big to get out a window. Rescuers had to smash an outside wall of the building and then use a block and tackle to lower her to the ground. It took 18 men on the end of the rope to get her down.

Anna went back to Nova Scotia, where she met American giant Martin Van Buren Bates, about two inches shorter than she was, and fell in love with him. The pair married and had two children. One was stillborn and the other lived only about 11 hours. Both babies were enormous. The first, a girl, was as large as her mother had been at birth, and the second, a boy, weighed in at just under 24 pounds and was 30 inches long. The giant couple stopped touring in circus shows about 1880, and Anna died of consumption in Ohio in 1888.

CHAPTER NINE

SCOTCH INC.

For around 100 years, Canada offered the Scots opportunities they would never have had in their homeland. The Scots grabbed those opportunities with such vigour that they came to dominate life in Canada, holding on with a vise-like grip that has only recently been loosened.

Canada became part of the British Empire at the right time for the Scots. They were just beginning to recover from the effects of the shotgun marriage with England forced on them by the 1707 Treaty of Union. The English made no secret of the fact that they had bribed the members of the Scottish Parliament to vote for the treaty, and Scotland had been crippled economically by an English-dominated joint parliament that did not hesitate to change the rules and ignore the 1707 treaty when it looked like it would favour Scottish interests. The only economic activities that thrived were based on Englishmen exploiting Scottish natural resources. (Does this ring a bell for anyone in a more modern, perhaps North American, context?)

Politics in Scotland were stagnant. Scottish MPs in the London Parliament had little influence over what was happening in their own country and could only hope that the English would appoint them to be one of the handful of managers used to run Scotland. The only way to get one of those appointments was to put English interests first. As late as the 1760s, the London mob felt its duty was to harass any Scot it could identify on the streets of the capital. Salvation and hope for the ambitious Scot lay across the Atlantic. The English had their hands full exploiting the New England states, so when New France was handed over to Britain in 1763, a wonderful blank canvas became available for Scottish enterprise.

The English wanted to swap the newly acquired territory along the St. Lawrence for the sugar-rich French-held island of Guadeloupe in the Caribbean, but the Scots wanted to keep Canada. In 1760, the *Glasgow Journal* wrote a rare editorial urging Scots to grasp the opportunities offered by the seizure of Canada with both hands. It's worth quoting part of that editorial. "The expense of this Conquest is the most thrifty disbursement ever made—an exclusive fishery! boundless territory! the fur trade engrossed! innumerable tribes of savages contributing to the consumption of our staple! There are sources of exhaustless wealth! Ignorant and designing men have called this a quarrel for a few dirty acres of snow, but the public will soon have feeling proofs that Britain must sink or swim with her colonies."

The businessmen and merchants who controlled the *Glasgow Journal* knew all about North America and its potential. They were the only people making any real money in Scotland before Union, when it was illegal for Scots to trade with England or English colonies. Years of punishing English duties on Scots goods had made the merchants expert smugglers, and Newfoundland, with its long rugged coastline, was a smuggler's paradise. Some Scottish merchants exploited a loophole in English law by setting up a base on Newfoundland, which England did not consider a colony. Registering their ships in the English town of Whitehaven added to the confusion and put the Scots in a good position to trade with English colonies in New England and the Caribbean. Scots sent salted fish from Newfoundland to New England, and rotten fish to the Caribbean to feed the slaves working on the sugar plantations. In return, tobacco and sugar from the Caribbean flowed back to the merchants on the west coast of Scotland, who then sold the goods in Europe.

After Union, Scottish merchants were quick to follow the British Army to the Maritimes when Acadia was wrested from the French. There was money to be made feeding and supplying the British garrisons, and rich cargoes of New Brunswick timber were just waiting to be shipped back to Scotland. It wasn't long before the Scots dominated the business communities of Halifax and St. John.

Along the St. Lawrence River, the economic engine was fuelled by fur rather than timber, but although the Scots dominated the collection and shipping of pelts, the furs were sent to London. The Scottish branches of the Montréal fur-trading partnerships were forced to send family members to London to protect their interests.

Scots business success in Canada owed much to family ties. Business in the 18th and 19th centuries was all about trust, and who can you trust if you can't trust family? Cousins and nephews were soon streaming across the Atlantic Ocean to run the Canadian offices of the Scottish trading houses that worked the Canada-Scotland-Caribbean triangle. The young men had little cash in their pockets, but they had ambition, determination and all-important family contacts. The Scots also tended to be better educated than their English counterparts and were thus able to make themselves more useful. To this day, the English regard a good education as something only the rich should have. Merit was more likely to be recognized and rewarded in Scotland than in England, where promotions were closely tied to parentage. And because so many of the leading businesses in Canada were Scottish, the country offered more opportunity than England did for an ambitious Scot with an eye to the main chance.

While some Scotsmen really did become millionaires after turning up on Canadian shores with nothing but the clothes on their backs and a few cents in their pocket, most of the future giants of Canadian commerce had something more—a letter of introduction or even a job offer from a friend or relative. Scots whose relatives weren't bosses often found themselves working for people from their hometown back in Scotland. In 1824, for example, the biggest shipping company in the world was Pollock and Gilmore, whose wealth was derived from its Nova Scotia operations. For two generations, Pollock and Gilmore was run almost entirely by people from the tiny Scottish parish of Mearns in Renfrewshire.

Different regions of Scotland tended to dominate different areas of the Canadian economy. Men from

Inverness, Aberdeenshire and Greenock ran the once-proud Canadian shipbuilding industry.

The Scots helped each other in business against outsiders, but they were fiercely competitive among themselves, and few dynasties lasted long unchallenged by other Scots. One of the few sectors to buck this trend was the Montréal fur trade. Its leaders tended to come from a few intermarried families originating in the Inverness area. The Frasers, McGillivrays, McTavishes, Smiths and Simpsons all came from an area within a day's coach ride of the Highland capital.

New Brunswick's timber trade and commercial salmon fishery of the late 1700s was dominated by men from the Inverness and Aberdeen areas. The timber business got a shot in the arm when the French Revolution plunged Europe into almost 20 years of constant war. At a time when the Royal Navy was crying out for new ships, the conflict cut Britain off from its traditional source of timber in the Baltic. Inverness man William Davidson got a contract to supply the Royal Navy with masts cut in New Brunswick, while fellow Scot James Dunlop, in Montréal, was making a huge 700-percent profit selling Canadian oak to the Scottish shipbuilders of Leith. In 1807 alone, 156 ships carried away 24,000 tonnes of New Brunswick timber.

The extended period of warfare also offered less reputable ways to make money, and Scots merchants in Halifax, such as Aberdeen man John Black, were quick to exploit them. One of the biggest rackets was auctioning off captured ships and cargo brought into Halifax by the Royal Navy. Men with inside information of the kind Scots naval officers were able to provide could make a killing. The War of 1812 offered the chance for some profitable smuggling operations via

British-occupied ports in Maine, and the Scots in Halifax and New Brunswick didn't let this opportunity pass.

Gradually, Scots trade with Canada became concentrated in the hands of the merchants operating along the banks of the River Clyde between Glasgow and Greenock. As early as 1763, brothers James and Robert Finlay were operating a regular cargo service linking the Clyde and Québec. Woolens, liquor, pig-iron and other manufactured goods were carried to Canada by ships that returned carrying lumber and potash (which was used to make glass and in the chemical processing of textiles). By 1785, nearly all Canadian imports to Britain were coming through Greenock.

The Industrial Revolution in Britain meant that Scottish businessmen were looking for a market to sell their mass-produced linen, cotton, iron and coal, and Canada fit the bill. Between 1763 and 1823, there were no fewer than 275 Scottish-based trading companies operating in Canada. These companies came and went, and few remained dominant for more than two generations as fresh waves of Scots were constantly arriving with more up-to-date business connections in Britain, the Caribbean and the Mediterranean than their longer established Canadian-born cousins.

Scottish societies in Canada were key to the networking that is so important to the business world. One of the first societies, the North British Club, was founded by Glasgow merchant Alexander Brymer in Halifax in 1768. (North Britain was the name supporters of the 1707 Treaty of Union tried to foist on Scotland.) The North British Club, like nearly all its imitators, provided a primitive social-welfare safety net for the poor, but all members were keen to make sure their charity dollars only went to the "deserving poor." The Scots were not keen on either giving or taking handouts. The annual report of the St. Andrew's Society of Toronto in 1888 went out of its way to stress that none of its charity money was going to "dead beats."

Sunday church services provided another excellent opportunity for networking, and the Scottish churches of Montréal attracted many worshippers who, though not Scots, were successful businessmen. By 1875, the Church of Scotland was the largest single Protestant denomination in Canada, a fact that is all the more surprising when you realize that, at the time, being Scottish could result in stigmatization. Not everyone appreciated the way the Scots networked with each other. In 1805, Irish-born judge Robert Thorpe branded them a "shop keeper aristocracy," and in 1847 the Reverend William Proudfoot, leader of the United Presbyterians, lamented, "We are too Scotch—our habits, our brogue, our mode of sermonizing are all too Scotch." It is no wonder, perhaps, in the face of prejudice from the English, Irish and Canadiens, that the Scots tended to stick together and look after their own.

The presence of so many Scots in the upper echelons of Montréal society for so long irks some extreme Québécois nationalists to this day. Every francophone in Montréal claims to have at least one grandparent who was instructed to "speak white" in one of the big downtown department stores. It is no surprise, then, that it was only after the Parti Québécois lost power that the province recognized World Tartan Day. Or perhaps it should be a surprise given the large number of Québécois with Scottish blood in their veins, some tracing back to the days of Abraham Martin in old Québec City or the Highland soldiers who settled in the province after 1763. The provincial motto, *Je Me Souviens*, "I Remember," reminds us that memory can sometimes be selective.

Almost without exception, the Caledonian and St. Andrew's clubs in various cities were firmly Tory in political conviction, and outsiders came to regard them as bastions of privilege. Their Scots members knew when they were onto a good thing and didn't like to see anything interfere with the way they did business. But business was changing, and a lot of that change was bad news for the Scots. Undersea telegraph cables joined England and North America in the mid-1860s, and improved communication between Montréal and London meant that the branch offices the Scots ran in Canada were no longer so important. The English had also been working their magic in the London Parliament to handicap the innovative and well-run Scottish banking system. A financial services act passed in 1845 made London the financial capital of the Empire. Important loan and financing decisions regarding Canada that were once made in Glasgow and Edinburgh were now made in London, and the Scottish banks slowly withered.

Canadian banks had modelled themselves on their close Scottish cousins from day one. They followed the Scottish example of establishing networks of branch offices that issued shares to the public and offered generous (at least by the standards of the time) lending policies. Well into the 20th century, Canadian banks recruited their clerks in Scotland to trade on the Scots' reputation for financial shrewdness, thrift and honesty. One of the most famous Scots bank clerk imports was the poet Robert Service, who gathered the material for such classics as "The Shooting of Dan McGrew" while working in the Yukon.

Owning a bank was good business for the successful Scot in Canada, particularly since bank directors were unlikely to have loan requests turned down. When the Bank of Montreal was founded in 1817, it had five Scottish directors. Three more joined the board a year later. Scots made up more than half of the 25 directors of New Brunswick's Charlotte County Bank when it was established in 1832, and the commercial district of St. John was long known as Scotch Row.

While the Bank of Montreal pulled most of the financial levers in Québec, Ontario had the Bank of Upper Canada. Once again, Scots were heavily involved in setting it up. Huntly-born William Allan, one of the province's leading businessmen, was instrumental in establishing the bank in 1821. His connections to the notorious Family Compact, the tight-knit group that ran the province through its control of public appointments, ensured the licence to operate a bank went to Allan's group rather than his rivals in Kingston. Those connections with Ontario's self-perpetuating and self-appointed aristocracy allowed the bank to bend some of the rules regarding capital assets and to ward off competition from the Bank of Montreal.

Scots were also prominent in the insurance business, which, along with the banks, managed much of the investment capital available in Canada.

Even though the dice became increasingly loaded against the Scots' way of doing business as the 19th century closed, they were still big players. The 1910 Canadian census revealed that 30 percent of the top 175 industrialists in Canada had a father born in Scotland. The figure included industrialists born in

Scotland and those born in Canada with a Scottish father, but not those second-generation Canadians who regarded themselves as Scots. Only 14 percent of the population in 1910 was classed as Scottish. (Interestingly, if a person's ethnic origin had been determined in the census through the mother rather than the father, several of the "Scots" in the fur trade and western Canada would have been listed as Natives.)

Among the 175 leading industrialists was Hugh Montagu Allan, the son of shipping millionaire and would-be railroad baron Sir Hugh Allan. The younger Allan managed to keep the family fortunes intact and merged his father's Merchants' Bank of Canada with its old rival, the Bank of Montreal. He also served on the board of directors for Canada Steamship Lines, the Royal Trust Company, Ogilvie Flour Mills and the Montreal Light, Heat and Power Company. Allan was unusual in that he had more daughters than sons killed by the Germans during the First World War. Two of his daughters were drowned when their ship was torpedoed off the coast of Ireland in 1915, and his only son was killed while flying as a Royal Navy pilot in 1917.

The Ogilvie Flour Company proved almost as controversial as that other Scot-dominated Canadian colossus, the Canadian Pacific Railway. It played a crucial role in opening up the West after a lucky piece of war profiteering. Alexander Ogilvie came to Québec in 1800 and within a year was in the milling business. In 1854, the Crimean War between Britain and Russia cut off England's supplies of Ukrainian wheat, and the Ogilvies stepped in to fill the gap in the market with Canadian grain. They invested their profits in bringing the latest steel-roller technology from Hungary so that they could mill a superior grade of flour. By 1877, the

Ogilvies were shipping wheat out of Manitoba. They had a mill in Winnipeg five years after that.

The Ogilvies earned the hatred of western grain growers as a result of a deal offered by Canadian Pacific. CP promised that once a company built a steam-powered grain elevator at any point on its line, the railway would no longer load grain into its rail cars there from farmers' wagons or non-mechanical storage bins. This meant the farmers had to sell to the elevator operator at whatever price the operator offered. Soon the CPR and the Ogilvies, who had the most grain elevators in the west, were accused of running a monopoly. Records show that the Ogilvies' agents on the prairies were indeed cheating the farmers in 1884-85. (It's not known if one of those farmers was William Dalrymple, whose 30,000 acres of wheat in Manitoba took almost a month to harvest using 450 labourers and 75 reaping and baling machines.)

Of course, not all of the Scots who arrived in Canada became business tycoons. The vast majority came here because the sweat of their brow paid better in Canada than in overcrowded and frequently economically depressed Scotland. Most of the Scottish immigrants were skilled workmen, and Scots stonemasons were particularly sought after. With their skills, the Scots also brought an attitude that some people describe as a strong sense of social equality and others describe as arrogant bloody-mindedness. It is no surprise that many Scots became involved in the union movement.

The miners of Cape Breton and their counterparts in the steel and iron works of Sydney were especially noted for their militancy and determination. One of the miners' strongest leaders in the late 1800s was

Greenock-born Robert Drummond of the Provincial Workmen's Association of Nova Scotia. Drummond shared his countrymen's belief in self-improvement and a fair day's pay for a fair day's work. When the mechanisms of coal-mining capitalism infringed on the working man's right to a fair return for his sweat, Drummond went after the bosses like a Highland terrier going for a rat. He first took on the mine owners at Spring Hill in 1878 when they cut miners' pay by six cents per box of coal cut.

Over the next two decades, Drummond was involved in 70 strikes. He liked to quote Scots poet Robbie Burns and lines from Shakespeare during negotiations with the mine owners and always tried to show the bosses that his union was not a thinly disguised criminal organization bent on extortion, but a moderate force for change and the common good.

Drummond's personal motto was "None cease to rise but those who cease to climb," and he certainly died a rich man through his investments. Drummond was accused of selling out when he supported the creation of the giant Dominion Coal Company and the British Empire Steel Corporation, which between them controlled Cape Breton's industrial well-being, but he believed that only big concerns could survive in the North American market, and the two industrial giants represented a partnership between business and the provincial government. As far as Drummond was concerned, the coal was not the company's coal but the people's coal, and the province's involvement meant the company's profits would contribute to the common wealth. Another indication of his socialist leanings was his campaign to have the vote extended to all men and women in Nova Scotia. The fight for male enfranchisement was successful, but Nova Scotia women did not win the right to vote until 1918.

Drummond hated the United Mineworkers of America (UMA), which set up shop in Cape Breton in 1917. He believed the UMA was an American fifth column whose real agenda had nothing to do with the welfare of the working man in Nova Scotia. Drummond probably wouldn't have got on well with Glasgow-born miner James Litterick, whose instructions came from Moscow. Litterick was a member of the Communist Party before he came to Canada from Scotland in 1925 (the same year Robert Drummond died). In 1934, his Russian masters chose him to be secretary of the Communist Party of Manitoba, and two years later he was elected to the provincial legislature to represent a working-class Winnipeg riding. He lasted until 1940, when he was expelled from the legislature after the Communist Party was outlawed. The Royal Canadian Mounted Police made a big deal of looking for him, but he vanished from public view. Some people now believe that he was actually a spy for the Mounties, and when his fellow Communists discovered this, they murdered him and threw him into BC's Fraser River.

Of course, just as every Scot who came to Canada did not became a millionaire, not all of the Scottish miners in Canada were socialists. Robert Dunsmuir was one canny and ruthless Scot who came to Canada with only the clothes on his back and died a millionaire. He was brought out from Kilmarnock in 1851 by an uncle who was the foreman at a Vancouver Island mine owned by the Hudson's Bay Company. Shortly after he arrived, the mine near Port Hardy was closed and the workers were given jobs at the company's Nanaimo operation. When the miners at Nanaimo went on strike, Dunsmuir refused to join them. The HBC rewarded him with a licence to work an abandoned coal shaft. The HBC sold the Nanaimo mine to the Vancouver Coal Mining and Land Company (VCM&L) in 1862, and the new owners hired Dunsmuir as a supervisor. He quit two years later to work in a small independent mine financed by Royal Navy officers stationed on the island, but as a result of financial problems it was sold to VCM&L.

The Vancouver company gave Dunsmuir his old job back but didn't realize he was spending his spare time searching for new coal seams to develop himself. When he found the richest coal seam on Vancouver Island, only five miles northwest of Nanaimo, he went back into partnership with the Royal Navy officers to work it. Dunsmuir insisted on holding half the shares in the new mining company and retaining complete operational control. By 1879, he was running the biggest mine on Vancouver Island and was busy buying out his partners. His sons James and Alexander worked alongside Dunsmuir for years, learning the mining business, and were partners in what had now become strictly a family concern.

When he was faced with a strike in 1877, he locked his workers out. The police and militia were then brought up from Victoria to harass the miners until they agreed to return to work—for a lot less pay than they were getting before the strike. Dunsmuir preferred to employ Chinese immigrants in his mines because they would work for half what anyone else would, and by the 1880s, Chinese men made up at least 50 percent of his workforce. Because Dunsmuir was an expert miner himself, his mines were safer than most. But that didn't stop him fighting any safety legislation tooth and nail.

Dunsmuir was soon the coal king of BC, with his own fleet of ships to move the black stuff, but a grateful province was about to make him even richer. In 1883, Dunsmuir was asked to build a rail line between Nanaimo and Victoria. His price was a $750,000 subsidy, two million acres of land on Vancouver Island, including the mineral rights, and permission to cut as much timber as he needed for the railway construction. It was a massive surrender of the province's natural resources to one man.

Dunsmuir died in 1899 and did not live to see his son James become premier of British Columbia the next year. His empire was sold to Scots-Ontarian railroad men William Mackenzie and Donald Mann in 1910.

Early in the 20th century, Scottishness came to be seen as more than a business asset by some Scots. They believed it was a bulwark against Yankee individualist materialism. In 1903, Alexander Fraser, a businessman, journalist and founder of the Gaelic Society of Canada, called for Scots in Canada to do more to promote their culture as a source of national unity. "Broadly speaking," he declared, "our duty as Canadian citizens, and as citizens in full standing of the British Empire, is clear—to do what in us lies to advance the common weal, to strengthen ties which bind us to the land we left and the land we live in, by every worthy means available, and in this way to build up a national ideal which our offspring can pursue."

One thing Scots and Canadians share is a belief in universal health care. Some say a society can be judged by the way it looks after its young, old and sick. The Scots, both at home and abroad, have always believed in self-improvement, advancement based on hard work and merit, and self-reliance. But that belief is always tempered by a recognition of community responsibility and the value of contributing to the common good. Today the Scots spend more per head on health care than their English cousins. (Does that remind you of another nation, south of another border, that shows a less-than-generous attitude to its sick?)

The Scots fought long and hard to keep the United States out of Canadian business. Prime Minister Sir John A. Macdonald and his Scots Tory backers fought a successful election campaign in 1878 on an anti-American-imports ticket. As far as Macdonald was concerned, American free trade was in reality unfair trade. Of course, keeping cheap American goods out of the hands of Canadian consumers was good for Scottish business. But then again, having been pushed out of one homeland by the commercial imperialism of a southern neighbour, perhaps the Scots were more sensitive than most to the issues involved. Today's Scots and Canadians are both very familiar with the phrase regarding a mouse in bed with an elephant.

It seems strange, in view of the Scots business community's almost solid support for Macdonald's National Policy, to learn that only 29 years earlier some of its leaders were advocating Canada's voluntary annexation to the United States. The Scottish stonemason-turned-canal builder John Redpath, president of the Montreal Annexation Association, was one of many of his fellow countrymen who believed the London Parliament did not have Canada's interests on its radar. That English-dominated Parliament, anxious to find the cheapest suppliers in the world, cast aside trade arrangements that made it economical to ship Canadian goods to Britain. As a result, the Canadians looked to America as a trading partner, but the Americans imposed a 20-percent customs duty on Canadian goods. It seemed that the only way to access markets in the United States was to join the country. When the London Parliament was also quick to sacrifice Canadian interests in treaties aimed at appeasing the Americans, some people thought it likely the British were about to sell Canada to the Americans. The annexationists could not lose. Either they would negotiate a better annexation deal with the Americans than the British were prepared to do, or the London Parliament would have to take Canadian interests more seriously.

As it turned out, the annexation movement was a wake-up call for the British, and the need for it faded. In the Reciprocity Treaty of 1854, the British governor general, Lord Elgin, gave Americans access to Canada's East Coast fishery in exchange for the removal of U.S. customs duties. Elgin was enough of a politician and realist to see how the American system of government worked. He hired a "fixer" in Washington, Israel de Wolfe Adams, and gave him a budget of $118,000 to ensure the trade treaty was passed. No fewer than 90 people in the U.S. capital received donations from Adams. Redpath was also a winner thanks to the trade treaty, and he began building Canada's first sugar refinery in 1854.

Not all Scots in Canada agreed with Redpath's flirtation with the United States, but nearly all agreed on the need for Canada to give young Canadians access to a university education based on the Scottish broad-curriculum model. Several Scottish-style universities were established throughout eastern Canada, but McGill University in Montréal attracted most of the Scots' money. Glasgow-born fur trader and land speculator James McGill had gifted 46 acres of land in Montréal and £10,000 for the establishment of a university that he insisted must bear his name. Redpath, the Ogilvies, Donald Smith and tobacco millionaire William MacDonald were all on the university's long list of Scots benefactors. Another McGill, who wasn't really a McGill at all, also contributed money to the university. Financier Peter McCutcheon from Galloway changed his name to McGill to inherit his uncle John McGill's money. McGill Street in Montréal is named for him rather than the university founder.

The men who funded McGill University and who benefited from the booms of the middle to late 19th century, when the Scots really ran Canada, had established themselves in the decades before. In some cases their sons, grandsons and even great-grandsons kept the family fortunes afloat into the 1960s, but the Scottish links were fading year by year. By the end of the 19th century, the Scottish influence over the Canadian economy was dwindling, and it was more difficult for fresh-faced Scots to become millionaires after arriving in Canada with nothing in their pockets but a letter of introduction to a relative. Scotland itself had become a branch-plant economy, and it served no purpose to maintain business connections there. The world of business was now based on a model far different from the one that revolved around the counting houses of Greenock, the coffee shops of Halifax and Montréal and the virgin forests of British North America.

STOP THE PRESSES

There was a time when the Scots had a lock on the mass media in Canada. Before radio and television came along, most people got their news and information from newspapers, and there were few places in the old Dominion of Canada that didn't have a newspaper with a Scot editing it.

A wag once remarked that while Parliament made the decisions, the debate was held in the press. Scot William Lyon Mackenzie, a republican agitator and the sworn enemy of the Family Compact in the 1830s, preached his gospel through his newspaper, the *Colonial Advocate*. Fellow Scot George Brown used his *Globe* in Toronto to push the case for Confederation in the 1860s.

One of Brown's protégés was John Robertson, who founded the *Toronto Telegram* after leaving the *Globe*. Robertson was a true newshound and once brought the *Globe* 150 stories in one day. But he preferred short, crisply written stories to the long-winded preachy rants of the *Globe* and was quick to leave when he had the chance to become co-owner of Toronto's first evening newspaper, the *Telegraph*, in 1866. The newspaper got a big boost when Robertson covered the first Riel rebellion at Fort Garry in 1869 and wowed his reading public with his breathless eyewitness reports of events there. However, a falling-out with the Tory party, which was angry at the independent stance of the newspaper, meant the *Telegraph* lost its financial support, and it folded in 1872. Brown took Robertson back, but in 1876 he started up the *Toronto Telegram*, a paper aimed at "the masses and not at the classes." Robertson kept the price of the paper and its advertising space low, and it ended up being the best-selling paper in Toronto by the 1880s. He was also a tight-fisted union-buster who liked to keep his employees virtuous by paying them little and working them long hours. His policy of encouraging readers to believe that his paper was the peoples' champion while at the same time treating his own workers badly is a tradition continued in Canadian newspapers to this day.

One man who would have had little time for Robertson was Edinburgh-born Bob Edwards. The Alberta journalist created a newspaper in 1903 that is still a legend in western Canada. The *Calgary Eye Opener* was a deliberate blend of clever satire, social crusading, risqué jokes, sports coverage, savage editorials slamming the antics of the rich and powerful, and witty one-liners. Edwards realized early on that to get enough readers for his serious journalism about corrupt politicians and other swindlers, he needed to attract people who would buy the newspaper mainly for the off-colour jokes and sports coverage. He once ran a "Wreck of the Week" column as part of a campaign to persuade the Canadian Pacific Railway to improve safety at level crossings. By 1908, the *Eye Opener* was selling 18,500 copies, including 4000 in Toronto, 2600 in Winnipeg and 1000 in Vancouver. Edwards was also selling 1800 on the CPR's trains—despite the "Wreck of the Week" feature.

Edwards championed the interests of Alberta's working people, even the prostitutes, in his newspaper and was also good for a personal handout to folks he felt were genuinely down on their luck. Shortly before his death in 1922, Edwards urged a friend to take $5 from his wallet to give to a man who had just lost his job. The Scot was known to all, from street bum to city lawyer, as "Bob." He made no secret of his liking for hard liquor, and it wasn't unheard of for Edwards to shut the

Eye Opener office for a week or so to go on a drinking spree or a fishing trip. After he was elected to the Alberta Legislature in 1921 as an independent candidate, he made only one speech. It was a criticism of Prohibition, which had been implemented in the province in 1916.

Scots Canadians also revolutionized journalism back in Britain. Max Aitkin produced his first newspaper as a 13-year-old in New Brunswick. He went into the world of finance as a young man, but after making his fortune he headed to Britain, where he was an associate of a fellow New Brunswicker of Scots descent, Andrew Bonar Law. (Law was the only Canadian to become British prime minister.)

In Britain, Aitken returned to his first love, newspapers. Using the money he'd made in Canada, he began buying failing titles and turning them around. His media empire really took off when Aitken acquired the *Daily Express* during World War I and transformed a dull newspaper into a dynamic product that caught the public imagination. By 1934, the *Express* was selling 1.7 million copies a day, and shortly after World War II it was the best-selling newspaper in the world, with a daily circulation of 3.7 million. Max Aitken was a hands-on owner and ruthlessly used his newspapers to promote his own political ambitions.

The second Scots Canadian to have a major impact on the British media business was Roy Thomson, who was almost the exact opposite of Aitken when it came to interfering with his editors. Thomson trusted his editors to know what their readers wanted and then to squeeze every penny of profit out of his media empire through tight-fisted financial micromanagement. After building up a newspaper and radio chain in Canada, Thomson returned to his Scottish roots by buying the historic *Scotsman* newspaper in Edinburgh in 1952. He also created the first commercial television station in Scotland, Scottish Television, though he later regretted describing his Scottish TV franchise as "a licence to print money" because it gave the impression he was overcharging his advertisers. Thomson went on to acquire the *Times* of London, required reading for the English ruling classes, and the *Sunday Times*, which pioneered investigative journalism in Britain under his ownership in the 1960s.

The last Scot to make any noticeable impact on the Canadian media was Vancouver-based radio and television pundit Jack Webster. The abrasive and opinionated Webster made much of his upbringing in Glasgow and his early days as a newspaper reporter there to project an image as a no-nonsense, straight-talking tough guy. He came to Canada in 1947 and immediately landed a job at the *Vancouver Sun*, where he attacked local trade unionists as communist saboteurs. He jumped to radio in 1953, then went back to Glasgow in 1957 for a brief spell with Roy Thomson's Scottish Television. He returned to BC in 1963 and never looked back. From radio in New Westminster he went to television in Vancouver. He was soon seen across Canada as the man in Vancouver for CBC's current affairs program *This Hour Has Seven Days*. Later he moved to BCTV, but after he retired in 1987, he frequently appeared as a panellist on the CBC's popular game show *Front Page Challenge*. Webster died in 1999.

GUNS, PHONES AND OTHER SCOTTISH INVENTIONS AND DISCOVERIES

If you ask people to name a famous Scottish Canadian inventor, most of them will answer Alexander Graham Bell. But there is another Bell who made a contribution to Canada that was just as important, if not more so.

Without the Reverend Patrick Bell, the Prairie provinces might not have been developed the way they were. Bell invented the first practical mechanical reaper, and without his work it's doubtful grain farming on the Prairies would have been economically viable. Most of the machines prairie farmers used were versions of the American McCormick reaper, but the U.S. machine was almost certainly based on Bell's work. Bell first cut a harvest in Scotland in 1828 on his father's farm near Dundee, three years before Robert and Cyrus McCormick demonstrated their machine. There were at least four of Bell's horse-driven machines in North America when McCormick "invented" and patented the mechanical reaper. However, Bell failed to patent his machine and did not have the capital necessary to produce it commercially, so McCormick got all the credit.

Bell came to Canada in 1833 as tutor to the children of Adam Fergusson, founder of Fergus, Ontario, but he later returned to Scotland. Fergusson became a pioneer of mechanized farming in Canada.

The mechanical reaper is just one of many examples of bogus American claims of inventive genius. Another American "inventor," Thomas Edison, spent most of his time fighting patent battles rather than working in the lab. Edison bought the patent for the light bulb from Toronto men Henry Woodward and Matthew Evans. He also had to buy the patent for an improved light bulb, which was invented by Englishman Joseph Swann around the same time Edison was working on his.

It is small wonder, then, that Scot Alexander Graham Bell decided to move from Canada to the United States in 1871 to develop the telephone and protect his rights, given that there were so many American "inventors" on the prowl for genuinely innovative ideas. Edinburgh-born Bell originally became interested in what eventually became the first practical telephone through his work with the deaf. Bell's mother and wife were both deaf, and he wanted to create a gadget that would allow him to talk to them. Others had done a lot of the groundwork that created the technology for the telephone, but it was Bell who figured out how to turn electrical current into sound waves. The solution came to him while he was visiting his father in Brantford, Ontario, in 1874. Newspaper publisher George Brown of Toronto applied for a patent for Bell's new invention in London, while Bell's father-in-law filed the patent in New York only hours before an American rival submitted his own application. Bell's 1876 patent, one of 30 he filed between 1875 and 1922, was to prove the most lucrative in the history of invention.

It took a few more months for Bell to actually transmit words over the wire. The first phone conversation was a monologue to his assistant: "Mr. Watson, come here. I want to see you." He perfected the technology for the telephone back in Brantford in 1877, and then he spent almost 15 years defending his patent. The legal papers involved formed a stack nine feet high.

Bell was no great fan of the telephone and once tore one off the wall of his home because of its constant intrusion into his life.

Bell went on to make a wireless transmission using mirrors 16 years before Italian Guglielmo Marconi claimed to have invented radio. (Many regard Canadian Reginald Fessenden as the true father of radio. He became the world's first public broadcaster on Christmas Day 1906 when he played the fiddle and read the Bible to radio officers on ships off the U.S. coast.)

Bell became an American citizen in 1882—a very wise decision in view of his patent battles—but his heart remained in Canada, and he was buried there when he died in 1922. It was from the frozen waters off his home at Baddeck, Nova Scotia, that he staged the first airplane flight in the British Empire when the *Silver Dart* took to the air in 1909. The pilot, Douglas McCurdy, went on to become Canada's first licensed pilot and lieutenant-governor of Nova Scotia.

One Scottish inventor who was cursed by a generation of Canadians was Charles Ross. The rifle Ross designed and persuaded the Canadian militia to adopt as its standard weapon in 1903, when there were problems acquiring the British Lee-Enfield rifle, proved a disaster during World War I. It was an excellent target rifle, but its mechanism was too complicated and delicate for trench warfare, and the bolt would jam solid. Canadian soldiers found themselves kicking at the locked bolts as German troops swarmed toward them. Many Canadian soldiers quickly "acquired" Lee-Enfields, which fired the same ammunition as Ross's rifle, and Sir Douglas Haig, commander of the British Expeditionary Force, made the switch official in 1916. The Ross continued in service as a sniper's rifle into World War II.

Ross, the 9th baronet of Balnagown, was a bit of a rogue and often owed money, which he never repaid. At the age of 21, after a dispute with his mother over possession of the family's Balnagown Castle, he stopped up the chimneys of the castle to smoke her out of it. The design of his rifle was close to that of the Austrian Steyr rifle, and production at his Québec factory was plagued by poor workmanship. The Royal North-West Mounted Police were issued the rifle but managed to switch to more satisfactory weapons in 1906. However, Ross had powerful friends, particularly Sam Hughes, the minister of militia, which is why his rifle continued to be used by the military.

David Douglas, former estate worker for the Earl of Mansfield, often narrowly avoided death while seeking plant specimens in Canada in the mid-1800s. The Scone stonemason's son was largely self-educated and was a star pupil at the Glasgow Royal Botanical Garden. The Horticultural Society of London recognized his ability and sent him to Canada in 1822 to collect plant specimens. The collecting expedition was such a success that the society sent him on another trip, to the Pacific Coast, in 1824. By 1827, with the help of the Hudson's Bay Company, he had travelled throughout western Canada.

Douglas returned to the Pacific Northwest in 1830 and continued his collecting work, even though the combined effects of blowing sand and snow glare from previous expeditions had weakened his eyesight. Once, he plunged down a ravine and was not found for five hours. By 1833, he was completely blind in his right eye, but that didn't stop him from trying to reach Alaska by canoe as part of a planned journey back to Britain via Siberia. The canoe voyage ended in disaster on the Fraser River near Prince George when an attempt to shoot some rapids went wrong. Douglas and his guide were caught in a whirlpool but managed to reach shore. They were starving and broken men by the time they had walked to Fort Vancouver in the Oregon Territory. A year later, Douglas was found dead in Hawaii. He had fallen into a pit dug to trap wild cattle. The 35-year-old collector had been gored and trampled by a bull that had fallen into the trap. No one knows how Douglas came to fall into the same pit.

David Douglas collected and catalogued 7000 species of plants at a time when only 92,000 species had been identified worldwide. Canada's largest tree, the Douglas fir, is named in his honour.

Another forgotten but influential Scot in Canada was Daniel Wilson. The Edinburgh man came to Canada in 1853 to chair the department of history and English literature at University College in Toronto. He was already a respected archaeologist and an expert in prehistoric man, and he spent much of his time in Canada studying Native culture. He was surprised at the reception he got when, during a speech in Philadelphia, he announced that black people were not an inferior species of humankind. Wilson was only repeating the doctrine of 18th-century philosophers who had declared that variations in cultures and the development of societies across the world were the result of circumstances and not innate racial character or biological destiny.

Wilson also believed that Métis children tended to be healthier human beings than their parents. He argued against forcing Aboriginal people onto reserves, where they were treated as overgrown children unable to make decisions about their own lives. The Scot had reservations about educating men and women in the same university classrooms but was a strong advocate for women enjoying a higher education. He also fought hard to ensure that Canadian universities followed the Scottish model by teaching a broad range of subjects and offering practical courses that prepared students for professional careers. He believed English universities, which focused on only a few subjects, discouraged students from studying engineering and medicine and were little more than self-perpetuating bastions of privilege for the children of the rich.

For much of Wilson's time, women were allowed to attend classes at university in Toronto but could not sit the final exams. Scots-born Jennie Trout studied medicine at Toronto, but she had to transfer to the Women's Medical College in Pennsylvania to qualify as a doctor in 1875. She then returned to Canada and was the country's first female licensed medical practitioner. She ran the Therapeutic and Electrical Institute in Toronto, which specialized in treatments for women involving electricity. On a more practical level, she ran a free dispensary for the poor. For health reasons, she moved to Florida in 1882 but helped establish a medical school for women at Queen's University in Kingston.

Although the Soviets claimed they invented television, it was in fact invented by Scot John Logie Baird in 1924 after sales of the medicated sock he developed for people with congenitally cold feet failed to sell as well as he hoped. In 1928, he invented a colour television. (Other notable Scottish inventions include pneumatic tires, radar, fingerprinting, adhesive postage stamps, the bicycle, nylons, postcards, smallpox inoculations, the fax machine and the use of antiseptic in surgery.)

These are only a few of the many scientific and educational pioneers in Canada with Scottish roots. They demonstrate that one tiny country on the northern fringes of Europe produced more doctors, engineers, scientists and educators than anyone on earth would ever have expected.

Scots at Play

Sports are not invented in a day. But the Scots can safely take credit for the popularity of four major Canadian sports—hockey, golf, curling and basketball.

The origins of hockey are lost in the mists of prehistory. The idea that fun could be had from hitting a ball with a stick seems to have popped up in several different cultures over tens of thousands of years, and many people claim to have found ancient carvings that "obviously" show people playing some form of hockey. Among the most ancient games in Scotland is shinty. Not shinny, shinty—though the word "shinny" almost certainly comes from "shinty." The Scottish game is a wild ball-and-stick game played by teams of a dozen a side, and it is rare for a game to be played without blood being drawn. Does that ring any bells?

It is believed the first hockey games were played in Nova Scotia around 1800, just about the time when the province was filling up with Scots. What could be more natural then going out on the ice and attempting to play shinty? The Mi'kmaq also had a hockey-like game, and the sticks they used proved far more suitable than the narrow triangular blades on the traditional shinty stick. Some sports historians believe hockey owes its origins to the Irish game of hurley, which is a close cousin to shinty. Common sense suggests that, given there were far more Scots than Irish in Nova Scotia at the time, it was shinty they based their ice game on.

Certainly it was the Scots who introduced the game of hockey to folks in eastern Canada. By then, the players were wearing ice skates. Reports that English soldiers introduced the game are just plain wrong. The English had not played a ball-and-stick game for 300 years, though in the early 1800s they adopted a game they learned in India as field hockey. It makes no sense that English soldiers would be out on the lakes and rivers of Ontario playing hockey. The first organized game in Montréal, in 1875, involved skates and sticks from Nova Scotia (the sticks made by Mi'kmaq craftsmen) and was played according to rules based on the ones already in use in Halifax. James Creighton introduced the game to Montréal. Creighton is a good Scottish name. Creighton even has a link to the Stanley Cup. He played hockey in Ottawa for a team called the Rideau Hall Rascals (the team sometimes went by the name Rideau Rebels), which also included two of Lord Stanley's sons.

Another good Scottish name is Roddy McColl. He taught the Royal Military College cadets at Kingston how to play the game when they faced the students of Queen's University in 1886. The principal of the university at the time was George Munro Grant and one of his players was William Kerr. (Could those be two more Scottish names?) Once again, the sticks were ordered from Nova Scotia. Sadly, the Scots didn't retain their dominance of the game for long.

Golf is another game with many fathers. The Chinese recently claimed that they invented golf. Communists like to claim they invented everything. So, while there are many who claim to have invented golf, it was the Scots who made the game their own. Scottish professional golfers taught the modern game to the world in the late 1800s. The Montreal Golf Club opened its doors in 1873, and Québec City's club was founded a year later. Toronto got its first golf club in 1876. Canadians have followed the Scots philosophy that golf courses should be enjoyed by as many people as possible, and many communities have municipal courses.

The Chinese have yet to claim they invented curling. Or have they? Curling was popular in Scotland in medieval times, but when the mini-ice age that marked the time period in northern Europe ended, Canada became the home of curling. Scots found the frozen rivers and lakes of Canada perfect for sending rocks sliding along. The first club was created in Montréal in 1807. Soon Scots were seizing the chance to network on the ice across the country. Kingston had a curling club in 1820, Québec followed a year later, the club in Fergus opened in 1834, and Halifax, Galt and Guelph all established clubs in 1838. Toronto's club was founded in 1836.

Basketball is one of the few sports that can trace its origins to a certain place and date. The first game was played on December 15, 1891, in Springfield, Massachusetts, based on 13 rules written by James Naismith. Naismith was the son of Scots immigrants, and the rules he came up with for bored students at the YMCA International Training School were based on a game he played as a child in Almonte, Ontario. The physical education teacher also coached rugby at McGill University in Montréal and introduced the helmet to American football.

Besides creating games, many Scots are well known for just plain creativity. Sir Walter Scott, Robbie Burns, Robert Louis Stevenson, Sean Connery, Robert Carlyle, Ian Anderson, Mark Knopfler and Annie Lennox are just a few of the Scottish writers, actors and musicians you may have heard of. The following are some Scottish Canadians who have made their name on the international scene.

Eric McCormack, star of the hit television comedy *Will and Grace*, claims Scottish and Cherokee descent. He trained as an actor at Ryerson University's School of

Drama and went to the same high school as comedian Mike Myers.

Toronto-born actress Lexa Doig is best known for her role as the computer Rommie in the television science-fiction series *Andromeda*. Her father is part Scottish and her mother is Filipina. She has also appeared in the television series *Tek Wars* and *Stargate SG-1*.

Before his death, Canadian John Candy was one of the best-known actors in Hollywood. The outsized Candy's father, Sydney, was of Scottish descent, while his mother, Evangeline, was of mixed Scottish and Polish blood. He got his big break as a member of the Second City comedy troupe. His movie hits include *Spaceballs; Uncle Buck*; *Stripes*; *Planes, Trains and Automobiles;* and *Splash*. Candy died of a heart attack in 1994 at the age of 43.

Colin Mochrie, another graduate of Second City, was born in Kilmarnock, Scotland, in 1957. Mochrie first came to fame in Britain as a regular on the television comedy improvisation show *Whose Line Is It Anyway?* and also starred in the show when it transferred to American television. Mochrie has appeared in several television series, movies and commercials.

Dave MacIsaac is a well-known Cape Breton guitar player born in 1955.

Vocalist Rita MacNeil is one of Cape Breton's best-known musical exports. MacNeil was the best-selling country music singer in Canada in 1990. She also had her own series on CBC between 1994 and 1997.

Lawrence Gowan, a Glasgow-born rock musician, is best known as a singer with the band Styx. He attended the Royal Conservatory of Music, where he studied the piano. He enjoyed a successful solo career in the 1980s and '90s.

Geoffrey Kelly was born in Dumfries, Scotland, in 1956 but is usually based in Vancouver. He is best known for playing the flute and whistle with the bands Spirit of the West and the Paperboys.

Helen King was born in Dunfermline, Scotland, in 1972 and is best known for her many roles on children's television, including the cotton ball-like lead role in *Me Too!* on CBC TV, and as the voice of Fumiko and Lisa in Discovery Kids' *Jacques Cousteau's Ocean Tales*.

Callum Keith Rennie was born in Sunderland, England, in 1960, but his parents are Scottish and brought him to Canada when he was four years old. Rennie has appeared in the television series *Battlestar Galactica*, *Highlander*, *Due South* and *Da Vinci's Inquest*, and in such movies as *Double Happiness* and *Hard Core Logo*.

Rowdie Roddy Piper was born Roderick Toombs in Saskatchewan in 1954. The well-known pro wrestler adopted the kilted persona of Rowdie Roddy Piper for the ring.

Shirley Douglas is the actress daughter of former Saskatchewan premier Tommy Douglas and mother of Hollywood heartthrob Kiefer Sutherland.

The international movie star Donald Sutherland comes from a New Brunswick family with strong Scottish links. He's best known for his roles in the movies *MASH*, *Kelly's Heroes*, *Klute* and *Ordinary People*, but he is most often seen these days playing ruthless but ageing American politicians.

Jack Whyte is best known as the top-selling author of a series of novels that describe the adventures of King Arthur in the days just after Britain stopped being part of the Roman Empire. He was born in Renfrewshire, Scotland, in 1939 but has lived in Canada since 1967.

Robert Service, the balladeer of the Yukon gold rush, was actually born in Preston, England, in 1874, but he was sent north to Kilwinning in Ayrshire, Scotland, when he was five to be brought up by his paternal grandfather and three doting aunts. When he was nine, the boy was reunited with his parents after they moved to Glasgow. He became a bank cashier in Glasgow and immigrated to Canada, where he got a job with the Canadian Bank of Commerce. His eight years working for the bank in the Yukon provided him with material for his classic poems "The Shooting of Dan McGrew" and "The Cremation of Sam McGee."

Publisher John Maclean was the son of a Scottish minister. In 1911, he gave his name to popular Canadian news magazine *Maclean's*, which he had founded six years earlier as *The Business Magazine*. He also created the *Financial Post*.

Buddy MacMaster, one of the best-known Cape Breton fiddlers, was born in Timmins, Ontario, in 1924 to Gaelic-speaking parents. The family returned to Cape Breton in 1928. MacMaster combined a career as one of the most popular fiddlers in Canada with a job working on the Canadian National Railroad.

Murray McLaughlin, a Juno Award winner several times over, was born in Paisley, Scotland, in 1948 and came to Canada when he was five years old.

CHAPTER TEN

THE HEART IS HIGHLAND

I t has been said that there are more bagpipers in Canada than there are in Scotland. It could well be true.

Scots who come to Canada start doing things they would never have dreamed of doing when they still lived in Scotland. They go to Robbie Burns Day suppers in January, drive hundreds of kilometres just to attend a Highland games in July, or buy licence plates that proudly declare their Scottishness. Canadians with one great-great-grandparent from Auld Scotia's sod proudly don a kilt and join the parade. What is it that makes people in Canada want to be Scottish?

The Scots and Canadians have a lot in common. They don't want to be American, English or French. They live in harsh northern climes. While most Canadians have freezing winters to contend with, the Scots live under almost perpetually leaden skies that drop rain on them all too frequently. Both have southern neighbours bent on economic domination, whose cultures threaten to swamp them. Most Scots called for jury service are astonished to find there are 15 jury members on a Scottish jury and not the 12 they see on the diet of TV courtroom dramas they are constantly fed by the English-dominated so-called national media in Britain. Canadian television dramas can only hope for good overseas sales if they pretend to be American.

Both countries strive to create and maintain distinct identities in spite of increasing pressure to conform to a global culture driven by consumerism and conspicuous consumption. Teenagers in Toronto, Beijing, London, Glasgow, Boston, Bombay and Singapore all want to wear the same clothes and shove the latest iPod technology into their ears. They yearn to eat the same fast food and drink the same cola and coffee. This may say more about teens and the universality of humanity than anything, but many people are beginning to feel there must be more to life than designer jeans and cappuccino.

Being Scottish offers an alternative. You can't get more alternative to designer jeans than a kilt. And what about a leather kilt? Such things really do exist and go a long way to explaining the fun involved in being Scottish.

It's easy to be Scottish. A Scot is someone who believes they are Scottish. That's all it takes. Scotland, like Canada, is a nation of immigrants. Genetics and DNA mapping aren't as much help as they appear. None of the people who live on the beautiful Knoydart Peninsula in the western Highlands are descended from the people who lived there before the Highland Clearances. The descendants of the original people were shipped off to Glengarry County in Ontario around

200 years ago. A scientist who didn't know that could make an awful mess of DNA-based ancestral research.

Wave after wave of invaders have come ashore in Scotland since the last major ice age, which makes untangling a Scottish DNA strand a daunting task. The Scots are a mongrel people and like most mongrels are tougher and more adaptable than purebreds. The amusingly named Beaker People were in Scotland before the Picts. The Scots, who drove the Picts out of the western Highlands and Islands, arrived after the Romans had left. And the Romans probably left some little bambinos behind when they departed. (By the way, it's a myth that the Romans never conquered Scotland. They conquered the bits they wanted and left the economically barren northern mountains alone.) Anyway, many of the "Romans" were really Spanish, French or North African. Boatmen from what is now Iraq were stationed at both ends of Hadrian's Wall to stop people sailing around the massive border fortification. Then came Vikings, Anglo-Saxons, French Protestant refugees, Flemish weavers, Dutch women who married Scottish soldiers at the end of World War II, Lithuanian coal miners and several recent waves of Poles. About one in every five people living in Scotland today is descended from Irish immigrants who began flooding into Scotland after the potato famine in the middle of the 19th century.

The point is that bloodlines aren't important when it comes to being Scottish. What could be more Scottish than a fluency in Gaelic? But many Scots are amused by the fact that there are now East Indians living in the Gaelic-speaking heartlands who can converse in a language beaten out of the Scots' own grandparents in classrooms and schoolyards decades ago. The language of advancement has always been

English, and the sooner Highland youngsters learned to speak it, the better. The decline of Gaelic on both sides of the Atlantic is one of the many striking parallels between Scotland and Canada. Around the time of Confederation in 1867, Gaelic was the third language of Canada, after French and English. Before the Second World War there were still tens of thousands of people living in Cape Breton who used Gaelic as the everyday language of the home. Now the figure is measured in hundreds. The picture is the same in Scotland. Gaelic is the language of old people.

Many Scots musicians have looked to Cape Breton for inspiration. They believe the island has acted as a time capsule, preserving music and dance traditions that have become corrupted in Scotland. In fact, the Cape Breton folks, as all good Scots will do, have created their own music and dance by fusing the best of what they had with the best of what they found in their new home. Many fiddlers will say that Cape Breton tunes owe as much to French and Irish influences as they do to Scottish. Scots music experts agree that Cape Breton music is more exciting than its Scottish cousin, but it is also harsher, heavier and more aggressive. Young Cape Breton musicians, such as Ashley MacIsaac, are now taking the next step and incorporating influences from outside the island to create a new musical fusion. The same thing is happening in other parts of Canada. One of the most popular attractions at cultural festivals across Alberta is the fusion of driving African drumbeats and the skirl of the pipes produced when the Big Rock Pipe Band's Dave Trew guests with the Wajjo Drummers.

The Scottish influence on music in Canada goes well beyond bagpipes and fiddles. Country and western music owes much to the Scots tradition. Northern Scotland was once cattle country, and for centuries Highlanders drove their beasts hundreds of miles to market. When ranching became big business in North America, many of the descendants of those drovers found themselves working on the ranches of western Canada and the American plains. Many old cowboy songs were based on Scottish or Irish ballads that ranch hands adapted to recount the realities of life on the range. One classic, the "Railroad Corral," was originally sung to the tune of the Scots rebel song "Bonnie Dundee," but is now associated with the melody of the Scots whaling song "The Greenland Whale Fisheries." There is even a cowboy song in Gaelic. "O Mo Shoraidh leis a'Coigich (Farewell to Coigach)" was composed in 1910 in Montana by a homesick Achiltibuie man called Murdoch MacLean. The popular "Blood on the Saddle" owes much to the ballad of 13th-century Scottish bad guy Halbert the Grim.

Perhaps the loudest Scots contribution to Canadian culture is the pipe band. But those pipers and drummers marching and counter-marching at Highland games across the continent are not really a traditional feature of Scottish life—though I suppose they might be, depending on how long a thing has to be done before it is considered traditional. The Highlanders at the Battle of Culloden in 1746 certainly didn't march toward the line of British redcoats behind pipe bands. The clan chiefs had their personal pipers to set the Highlanders' pulses racing with their tunes, but when the fighting started, the musicians put their instruments aside to cleave some skulls with their broadswords.

The pipe bands we see today were inspired by the British Army. The English regiments had fife and drum bands to play them into battle, but the Scots preferred pipers. Resistance to the fifes varied from regiment to regiment and time to time, but most Scottish units had pipers. Sometimes they were on the army payroll; often the troops paid for them out of their own pockets. Eventually, the army stopped foisting fifes on the Scots and accepted they would march behind a pipe and drum band. So a tradition was born.

The glamorous kilted regiments were the shock troops of the British Empire, and many others sought to emulate them. When the 48th Highlanders of the Canadian militia was formed in 1891, one of the first things the regiment did, even before it had rifles, was form a pipe band. The Edmonton Caledonian Pipe Band, made up almost entirely of city police, volunteered en masse to go with the Princess Patricia's Canadian Light Infantry when it sailed for Europe at the beginning of World War I.

One of the reasons the British Army grudgingly accepted the pipers was that Queen Victoria had fallen in love with all things Highland. Her love had a profound influence in both Scotland and Canada. Victoria's husband, Albert, and their sons were often photographed wearing kilts. Soon everybody who was anybody in British society was looking for an excuse to do the same. Albert even designed a tartan carpet for the royal family's Highland hideaway at Balmoral. It was an incredible turnaround. Kilts had been outlawed almost 100 years earlier when the Highlanders were feared and despised by the rest of Britain. But the people who had once been a threat to national security were now brutalized paupers. Wearing tartan became trendy. The implications were the same as they would be if Canadians decided today that

Cree or Mohawk traditional dress should become the national costume.

Many people in Canada during the time of Queen Victoria had first-hand experience of the suppression and defeat of Gaelic culture; it was why they had been shipped to Canada in the first place. But the Highland-ization of Scottish culture, with its universal adoption of kilts, tartan and bagpipes as national symbols, developed in Canada at the same time as it did in the Scottish Lowlands and England.

The first Highland games in Scotland were held in the early 1780s in the Lowland town of Falkirk. The first in Canada took place about 30 years later. Several of the Canadian Highland games predate most of the Scottish ones. The Braemar Games, near Queen Victoria's Balmoral home, weren't held until 1832. Most of the oldest Scottish and Canadian games date back to the 1850s and 1860s, and Highland games as we know them today, with their strength events and piping and dancing competitions, are as much a Canadian invention as a Scottish one.

Highland games really took off in Canada during the 1980s, with the number jumping from 26 in 1982 to 70 by 2003. There are few major Canadian communities that don't host one now. Tens of thousands flock to the bigger events for an excellent family day out for Canadians of all backgrounds. Admission to the games doesn't cost a fortune, there are no millionaire athletes shutting down any opposition player who shows a glimmer of talent or imagination, and the sports are not dominated by commercialism and drug abuse—though it has to be admitted that there has been griping on both sides of the Atlantic about alleged steroid abuse in some of the strength events. But, generally, the games promote community values and friendly competition. Haggis hurling may never make the Olympics, but that doesn't mean it's not a legitimate sport.

Highland games in Canada have grown beyond a few competitions for people in kilts. Mini-towns of tents spring up on the games site, featuring clan societies and re-enactment groups. Clan chiefs, speaking with English private-school accents, are often brought across the Atlantic from their homes in suburban southern England as guests of honour. And it seems that a fair number of the Canadians who turn out to see their clan chief in the flesh may actually be family. This contradicts the long-held notion that clans were not families at all. For years, experts claimed that many people adopted the name of the local clan chief as part of local power politics. However, a recent DNA study of Clan Macdonald by some Oxford University researchers found 25 percent of Macdonalds appear to share a common ancestor, the Viking Lord of the Isles Somerled. The percentage of MacDougalls and Macallisters descended from Somerled proved even higher.

But, getting back to the Highland games, for years now, Canadian girls have been dominating the dancing competitions in Scotland. Perhaps that isn't a surprise, given there are something like 300 Highland dancing schools in Canada. The domination of dancers from Canada and, to a lesser extent, the United States has become so common that a few of the bigger Highland games in Scotland, such as the Cowal Gathering, have started staging events restricted to Scots-born competitors in a bid to give them a chance of a medal.

Canadian pipers also regularly outclass their Scottish cousins in competition. The Northern Piping Meeting in Inverness, the piping equivalent of the Stanley Cup final, usually includes a fair sprinkling of Canadians among the winners. At one time, piping was almost compulsory in some Canadian communities. In the early 1950s, Cape Breton man Malcolm Gillis told author Charles Dunn: "When I was young and we went anywhere to visit, they'd be passing the pipes around from one man to the next, and we'd all have to try a tune. Anyone who couldn't manage would be so ashamed of himself, he'd try to learn pretty quick."

Cape Breton is now capitalizing on its Highland heritage to bring in tourist dollars, much the same way Highlanders do in Scotland. The image being marketed in Cape Breton is of hardy, independent, pioneer farmers. There's no mention of the sons who became militant unionized steelworkers and coal miners. And there are other parts of the Canadian reality that are left out of the story. In 1947, a "Lone Shieling" was built on the Cabot Trail in Cape Breton. It is a reconstruction of the stone and turf houses the immigrants left behind in Scotland—not an example of the timber shacks they built for themselves in the wooded wilds of Cape Breton. Why not build one of each?

While Cape Breton celebrates its Scottish heritage, memories of other Scot contributions to Canadian culture are fading. It's hard to believe now how popular Scottish writers and poets were in Canada just over 100 years ago and how strong an influence they had. While much that was being written in England focused on the trials and tribulations of the rich in their socially isolated country houses (Charles Dickens and Thomas Hardy were two exceptions to this rule and, not surprisingly, they are still remembered today), the Scots tended to write about ordinary people. That may well be because more ordinary people in

Scotland could read, thanks to a better education system than the English enjoyed. Tales of everyday Scots battling the odds to succeed struck a chord with Canadian readers that English tales of who would marry who up at the squire's mansion did not. Scots writers Sir Walter Scott and Robert Louis Stevenson were both popular in Canada, and nearly every English-speaking Scots immigrant in the 19th century brought a copy of the poems of Robert Burns with them. The poet's message of the essential brotherhood and equality of man was what many immigrants wanted to hear in their new homeland. This was especially true for the farmers who came to Canada to escape the grasping hands of landlords back in Scotland.

Scott, Stevenson and Burns all had a lot of Canadian imitators who are best forgotten. But they also inspired a generation of Canadian writers. From 1843 onward, Scots-born Hudson's Bay Company employee Robert Ballantyne churned out hundreds of boys' adventure stories set in Canada. Ontario clergyman Charles Gordon, writing as Ralph Connor, wrote books in the early 1900s (including *Glengarry School Days*) that are still studied in schools. Hugh MacLennan made much of his Nova Scotia Scots heritage in his writings during the 1940s and even travelled to Scotland in search of his roots. MacLennan found the human-made emptiness of the Scottish Highlands far more disquieting than the natural stillness of the Canadian Barrens. Present-day Cape Breton writer Alistair MacLeod's work frequently draws on the Highland immigrant experience in Nova Scotia. In Scotland, he is considered a Scottish writer and his books sit in the Scottish section. Apparently, this does not please visiting Canadians, though it's supposed to be a compliment.

Scots in Canada were not slow to apply their talents to boosting the growing patriotic fervour and desire for a national identity that swept the new nation after Confederation. Canada's unofficial national anthem, "The Maple Leaf Forever," was written by Lesmahagow-born Scottish schoolteacher Alexander Muir in 1867 for a song competition sponsored by Montréal's Caledonian Society. It won second prize, and he spent $30 printing 1000 copies, which he hoped to sell. The venture made $4. It turned out Muir had failed to secure the copyright on his words and music, and an established music publisher turned it into a hit in 1871 without having to pay him a penny. The song was popular right up until the First World War but was never in the running as the official national anthem because it pretty much ignored Québec. Muir described Canada as the place where the "thistle, shamrock and rose entwine" but made no mention of the fleur-de-lys. His description of General James Wolfe as a "dauntless hero" also failed to win over many Canadiens.

The English words to "O Canada" were penned by the son of Scottish immigrants. Lawyer Robert Weir wrote the words in 1908 as part of the celebrations to mark the 300th anniversary of Québec City. There had been a couple of previous attempts to create an English version of the 1880 Canadien anthem, with music by Calixa Lavallée and French lyrics by Adolphe Routhier, but it was Weir's words that caught the public imagination. It wasn't until 1980 that "O Canada" was officially adopted as the national anthem.

Culture is constantly evolving. If it didn't, banging two rocks together beside a blazing fire would still be considered cutting-edge music. One of the most surprising things is how Scottish and Canadian culture have developed in parallel. In both countries the population moved from farms to urban centres and lost much of its culture. Families of Canadians and Scots who had spoken Gaelic for several generations lost their language when they entered the industrial workforce in their respective countries. But both peoples have retained a basic culture that differs from that of their southern neighbours, and they share a belief in certain key virtues—tolerance, good humour, toughness, honesty, a spirit of individualism tempered with good neighbourliness and a strong belief that hard work should be, and will be, rewarded. Even speech patterns are mirrored. Where many Canadians will end a sentence with "eh," a Scot will say "see." See?

The Scots have always had a fondness and respect for Canada. They see parallels to their own experience clearly. Those who came to Canada did so because they believed they would be allowed to build a kind of life that was impossible in Scotland. Many of them worked hard not just to improve themselves but also on behalf of their new homeland. They did not want to see the mistakes of Scotland's past repeated in Canada. The Scots wanted to come to Canada and didn't see it as a poor alternative to emigrating to the United States. Even during those periods when more Scots were going to the United States, the Scottish media focused on Canada as a destination for emigrants. For example, the *Aberdeen Journal* back in Scotland treated the first annual ball hosted by the Aberdeenshire, Banff and Kincardineshire Association of Winnipeg in 1911 almost as local news.

The Scots have certainly had a big influence on Canada, well beyond their numbers. Many different types of Scots have come to Canada in the last 300 years. Some, perhaps the majority, merged in seamlessly and quickly with nothing to suggest a Scots connection but a name beginning with "Mac." It really wasn't so long ago that immigrant kids were subjected to forced assimilation on the playgrounds of Canada and couldn't shed their Scottish accents quickly enough. Others played up their Scots connection for all it was worth. In his 1911 book *Scots in Canada*, J. Murray Gibbon counselled that "the best passport for any immigrant into Canada today is to speak with a Scots accent." Scots went down coal mines, got jobs in car plants, ploughed up the virgin prairie, traded furs in the Arctic, canned salmon, herded cattle, built ships, chopped down forests, preached the gospels, founded newspapers, paid bribes, took bribes and worked in widget factories. A few were snobs; most were working Joes with a strong belief they were inferior to no man. A handful were racists, but just as many were active in fighting for basic rights for everyone regardless of creed or colour.

There remains a strong Scots flavour to Canada. The Scots failed to make quite the same mark in other countries that attracted large numbers of British immigrants, which may be why Canadians are distinguished from Australians by more than their respective accents. Yes, there is something Scottish about Canada. But what is Scottish?

Almost 100 years ago, Wilfred Campbell wrote a book called *The Scotsman in Canada*. In it he mused, "men may rave of the heather, the hills, the pibroch and the Brig of Ayr, but all the time the real Scotland and the true Scottish people are a mystery to themselves and to others."

THE END

NOTES ON SOURCES

Barnes, R.M. *The Uniforms and History of the Scottish Regiments.* Seeley, Service and Co., 1956.

Blaise, Clark. *Time Lord.* Random House, 2000.

Bryce, George. *The Scotsman in Canada* Vol. 2. Musson, 1911.

Calder, Jenni. *The Scots in Canada.* Luath Press, 2004.

Campbell, Wilfred. *The Scotsman in Canada.* Musson, 1911.

Cruise, David, and Alison Griffiths. *Lords of the Line.* Penguin, 1989.

Douglas, Ann. *The Compete Idiot's Guide to Canadian History.* Prentice Hall, 1997.

Fry, Michael. *The Scottish Empire.* Tuckwell Press/Birlinn, 2001.

Gibbon, John Murray. *Scots in Canada.* Musson, 1911.

Harper, J.R. *The Fraser Highlanders.* The Society of Montreal Military and Maritime Museum, 1979.

Haydon, A.L. *The Riders of the Plains.* Hurtig, 1971.

Herman, Arthur. *How the Scots Invented the Modern World.* Crown, 2001.

Hill, Douglas. *The Scots to Canada.* Gentry, 1972.

Hollihan, Tony. *The Mounties March West.* Folklore, 2004.

Hunter, James. *The Making of the Crofting Community.* John Donald, 1976.

Hutchison, Bruce. *The Struggle for the Border.* Longman Canada, 1955.

Library and Archives Canada. *Dictionary of Canadian Biography Online.* www.biographi.ca/EN/index.html

MacEwan, Grant. *Eye Opener Bob.* Institute of Applied Art, 1957.

McLean, Marianne. *The People of Glengarry.* McGill Queen's University Press, 1991.

Morton, Desmond. *A Short History of Canada.* Hurtig, 1993.

Morton, Desmond. *A Military History of Canada.* Hurtig, 1985.

Mowat, Farley. *The Farfarers.* Seal, 1998.

Murray, John Wilson. *Memoirs of a Great Detective.* William Heinemann, 1904.

Newman, Peter C. *Empire of the Bay.* Penguin, 1998.

Norton, Wayne. *Help Us to a Better Land.* University of Regina, 1994.

Prebble, John. *Mutiny.* Penguin, 1977.

Rattray, W.J. *The Scot in British North America.* MacLean, 1881.

Ray, Celeste, ed. *Transatlantic Scots.* University of Alabama Press, 2005.

Reid, W. Stanford, ed. *The Scottish Tradition in Canada.* McClelland and Stewart, 1976.

Rider, Peter, and Heather McNabb, eds. *A Kingdom of the Mind.* McGill Queen's University Press, 2006.

Severin, Tim. *The Brendan Voyage.* Hutchinson, 1978.

Tanner, Ogden. *The Canadians.* Time Life, 1977.

PAUL COWAN

Paul Cowan is a journalism graduate from Edinburgh, Scotland, and a recent transplant to Canada. In both Canada and Scotland, this award-winning journalist has reported on crime, disasters, troop deployments to Afghanistan, sports, human interest and much more. He has also written extensively on the history of the Scots in North America.